Praise for *The Pare*

"This book is like having an occup

tic! Through science, step-by-step instructions, and helpful illustrations, Manela and Zwolinski beautifully reveal the secrets of therapeutic, purposeful connection for the benefit of parents and children alike. Let's dance, let's dance indeed!"

—Anthony T. DeBenedet, M.D., Coauthor of the Parenting Bestseller, *The Art of Roughhousing*

"The Parent-Child Dance offers many creative activities parents can do with their children at home to help them with some common behavioral issues. An additional benefit of these activities is the strengthening of the parent-child relationship."

—Howard Glasser, Executive Director of Children's Success Foundation & Creator of the Nurtured Heart Approach®

"Miriam Manela is a shining example of the type of compassionate and caring health professional that I recommend to parents. Her new book, *The Parent-Child Dance* could only have been written by someone with Miriam's expertise, dedication, and insight. In it, Miriam helps you get in touch with your child's inner world, and gives you the tools you need to strengthen your parent-child relationship without blaming or shaming."

—Richard M. Zwolinski, Anxiety and Addiction Expert, Author of *Therapy Revolution: Find Help, Get Better, and Move On (Without Wasting Time or Money)*

"The Parent-Child Dance is a wonderful resource book for parents and professionals to help children with the range of sensory processing disorders. This book is full of practical advice to help the child achieve better self-regulation, body organization, and sensory processing.

"The suggested activities and case examples specifically target children who experience irritability, anxiety, and are easily stressed, children with high activity level, as well as those with either sensory hypersensitivities or who seek and need sensory stimulation. This must-have book is full of activities that can be easily integrated into play and everyday routines."

—**Dr. Georgia DeGangi Clinical Psychologist, Occupational Therapist, expert in pediatric regulatory disorders, Author of *Effective Parenting for the Hard-to-Manage Child: A Skills-Based Book,* and other books.**

"Miriam Manela has the key to help you unlock the mystery of your child's challenging behavior. Whether that child is a heat seeking missile, a squeaky wheel or a child on the edge, in "The Parent-Child Dance," she shares simple techniques you can do at home to help give your child the skills he needs to adapt to a world he experiences differently than his peers. A compassionate, insightful, user-friendly book."

—**Pat Carroll, Morning Anchor, WCBS Newsradio Host, Host of "Raising our Kids", WCBS Radio**

"This elegant, easy to understand and practical book is a must-read for all parents, teachers and therapists who are seeking to elevate their consciousness as they develop relationships with children."

—**Kim Barthel, Occupational Therapist, Teacher, Author, NDTA OT Instructor and specialist in the fields of attachment and interpersonal neurobiology.**

"The Parent-Child Dance, by Miriam Manela, is a lovingly light book heavy with meaning and value. Ms. Manela suggests that "rather than seeing your child's behavior as antagonistic, think of it as a mystery to be solved." Her perspective focuses on sensory processing and integration, a core area of our life and functioning that is often overlooked by parents and professionals.

She provides us with ways of understanding children who are characterized by intensity or energy, as well as those who seem overwhelmed or who might be described as a 'squeaky wheel'. And she offers many sensory and interactive interventions to guide our children toward a centered, regulated, life where stress is met and managed with our guidance and support.

Here is a book for families with children who have sensory and behavioral challenges as well as for any family with children whose parents want them to thrive."

—Dr. Dan Hughes, Clinical Psychologist, developer of attachment-focused treatment that relied heavily on the theories and research of attachment and inter-subjectivity to guide his model of treatment and parenting.

"In Miriam Manela's new book, The Parent-Child Dance, she tells us that a child's behavior gives us clues into how he lives life, how he operates, and how he adapts to the world. The author opens a door for parents and explains what's really going on with your child, beneath the surface.

"She shows how various systems, especially the sensory system, work together to help your child function, and when they aren't working optimally, gives the reader numerous clinical techniques in the guise of play that can help your child's systems regain function."

—Daniel S. Samadi, M.D. Otolaryngologist with extensive expertise in treating ear, nose, throat disorders in children of all ages.

"What's really going on when your child is shut-down, angry, overly sensitive, or unable to sit still? In the Parent-Child Dance, occupational therapist Miriam Manela gives you the keys you need to understand your child's behavior—and gives you the tools you need to help him thrive. The simple and fun activities in this book will help a child who is "dysregulated" and has sensory-system challenges, but almost any child will benefit from the wisdom between these pages. Best of all, you can use this guide in conjunction with other therapies and treatments.

"Miriam's the kind of caring professional who's committed to helping parents and children in her well-known private practice; now, she's written a book so parents and children can benefit from her expertise in their own home.

"Miriam and I have worked together with many clients—and I recommend her for her professionalism, compassion, and expertise. Miriam gets results in challenging behavioral cases."

—Rabbi Sam Frankel, LCSW

From the foreword: "Miriam's dedication to her clients shines through in this book. So does her ability to embrace flexibility and avoid rigid prescriptions."

—Kelly Dorfman, Pediatric Nutritionist, Award-winning Author,
Cure Your Child with Food: The Hidden Connection between Nutrition and Childhood Ailments)

The Parent-Child Dance

A Guide To Help You Understand and Shape Your Child's Behavior

Miriam Manela, OTR/L
and C. R. Zwolinski

OT Thrive Publishing
Passaic, New Jersey
otthrive.com

ISBN: 0692249087
ISBN 13: 9780692249086

Illustrations by Dena Ackerman
Cover Design by Kathryn A. Van Horn

· Publisher: Miriam Manela, OT Thrive Publishing, Otthrive.com.

This book is dedicated to Kimberly Barthel, occupational therapist, teacher, author and my mentor, who gave me the tools to succeed. Every page has been influenced by her wisdom, and her knowledge of occupational therapy.

This book is also dedicated to Bernie and Goldie Kahn, my parents, for inspiring me by example and supporting me with their unwavering love.

Finally, this book is dedicated to my three beloved children—Boy, am I blessed!

Miriam Manela, 2014

Table of Contents

Foreword

I was so excited when Miriam asked me, a nutritionist, to write the foreword to her book on sensory processing. My first thought was, "Yahoo, she's got it!" After years of talking about how diet affects sensory system development, and in turn, how sensory processing affects what children eat, it is thrilling when it comes together in practice. As critical as the right therapy is for progress, even masterful intervention can fall flat if the body biochemistry does not support it. The best therapists (and I believe Miriam is one of them) recognize how much better their techniques work with a well-nourished child.

For over twenty-five years I have used targeted nutrition therapy to help people address their vexing symptoms. I am particularly interested in behavior, cognition, and development. My award-winning book, *Cure Your Child with Food: The hidden connection between nutrition and childhood ailments* (Workman, 2013), was written to help parents, teachers, and therapists recognize nutrition problems when they see them. You have much more control over the health and development of your children than you may realize. I have spread the word through radio and television appearances, writing for *Living Without* magazine and the *Huffington Post*, and giving workshops and talks all over the world. The right nutrition can make all the difference.

I became interested in partnering with occupational and speech therapists early in my career, when I noticed a big gap in my nutrition education. Pouring cheese on vegetables, or setting healthy food on the table and hoping that over time, the child would eat them, was not working for the kids I was seeing. They would be out the door or retching before the plate hit the table. Clearly, children with complicated behaviors and sensory processing problems required a multi-disciplinary approach.

Through the years, I've worked with a large variety of pediatric specialists and have had the pleasure of consulting on client cases with occupational therapist Miriam Manela. Miriam is an extraordinary collaborator. She has sat through nutrition consultations with families just so everyone is clear about the plan and on the same page. This is dedication far above and beyond the norm. She is consistently caring and incredibly compassionate with both parents and kids. When challenges arise, she jumps in with creative solutions and encourages families to persevere.

One case involved a young boy I will call Brandon. Though only six years old, Brandon was lethargic, overweight, and obsessed with food. Unfortunately, he was not obsessed with spinach or cucumbers, and avoided the healthier choices. I recommended adding a few nutritional supplements, as well as removing some foods that were triggering his excess appetite. The supplements were important because even though he was overeating, he was suffering from high-calorie malnutrition. That is, plenty of calories, but not enough vitamins and minerals.

We needed to close the gap between what he was willing to eat and what he needed for optimal development. Miriam knew therapy would not be successful until his significant nutritional issues were addressed. She recommended the family take on the dietary changes first, and then she began occupational therapy. This approach saved the family untold time and money. Once Miriam started treatment, Brandon improved rapidly and dramatically (and lost quite a bit of excess weight). The result was a grateful parent and a happy child. They would have been even more grateful if they truly knew how much they benefited from Miriam's innovative and flexible approach. I often get kids after months or even years of failed therapy. By that point, everyone is frustrated and cranky. In the saddest cases, there is no money left and/or the family is too discouraged to get the help they need.

Miriam's dedication to her clients shines through in this book. So does her ability to embrace flexibility and avoid rigid prescriptions. I particularly like the fact that *The Parent-Child Dance* offers alternative versions of many of the activities in the book, so parents can adjust for their child's abilities and preferences. Plus, the activities are fun! They give parents and children the chance to bond in play, which is so valuable to stressed-out, overbooked families. I really enjoyed the sensitive illustrations, which reflect Miriam's style. I also found the chapter titled "Taking Care of You" to offer a comforting reminder to parents: Perfection isn't possible. In this chapter, Miriam shares her wisdom, not only as a therapist, but as a loving parent of three boys of her own. Her insights into the importance of knowing yourself and how this is a key to good parenting, make this book essential reading.

I feel that these creative activities offer a way to help improve a child's behavioral issues, and therefore, his health and happiness. Though pediatric nutrition and occupational therapy are obviously quite different healthcare fields, they strive for the same goal: healthier and happier children, families, educators, and ultimately, societies.

Kelly Dorfman, MS, LDN
May 2014

Note to Parents, Guardians, and Professionals

The advice and suggested activities and interventions in this book are not to be considered a substitute for medical, psychological, therapeutic, or other professional advice. The authors, Thrive Occupational Therapy, and any persons associated with the writing, editing, or publishing of this book are not responsible for any accident or injury that may occur while trying the suggested activities or interventions in this book. Readers should regularly consult healthcare and other professionals in matters relating to their children's physical and emotional health, and particularly with respect to any symptoms that may require diagnosis or medical attention.

Introduction

Today, many parents are more actively engaged in raising their children than ever before. They're focused on giving their children the tools they need for adulthood: the best education and preparation for personal and professional life. They're focused on meeting their children's material needs, too, by giving their children healthy food, exercise, and other basic necessities of life. Although some of these parents may very well be considered "helicopter parents," hovering around their children trying to fill their every waking moment, the vast majority are not. They are simply good people doing their best at the most meaningful and hardest job in the world.

But for a variety of reasons, despite plenty of love and commitment, more children than ever are being identified as having some of these common emotional and behavioral problems: The Centers for Disease Control and Prevention says that over 9.5 percent of American children between the ages of 4 and 17 are said to have an Attention Deficit/Hyperactivity Disorder (ADHD)—that's over five million children. ADHD causes disruptions in learning, but also has a profound effect on home and family life, as well as a child's social life.

Today, anywhere from five to sixteen percent of children are said to have a sensory processing disorder. A sensory processing disorder may be any one of several disorders that may ultimately make it difficult for the child to experience everyday life in the way others do. It is a challenge for these children's brains to organize and appropriately respond to input from the environment, such as noises, movement, or smells.

Anxiety disorders also appear to be on the rise—and these can manifest a variety of startling symptoms, everything from extreme indecision to panic. Some of these children seem to be embroiled in constant conflicts—their anxiety is making most relationships combustible. According to the Anxiety and Depression Association of America, one in eight children are said to be affected.

And dyslexia, which is also prevalent, can cause kids not only to have problems with reading and writing, but also to "zone out" or be labeled "hyperactive," "class clown," or "troublemaker."

These problems can even overlap, but whether they do or not, they may cause children to do poorly in school, miss out on important social experiences, and struggle with relationships, including those with parents, siblings, teachers, and friends. Problems like anxiety and ADHD may even make children more prone to other disorders, like depression or substance abuse. But, it's important to remember that even the "average" child, who is "doing okay," can sometimes experience problems that lead to social confrontation, lack of interest in schoolwork, or other difficulties. Most parents I know are trying valiantly to think about their child's future—but are worried, frustrated, and overwhelmed trying to cope with their child's today.

•••

In my work as an occupational therapist at Thrive Occupational Therapy, the practice I founded in 2008, I help parents by helping their behaviorally challenged child. But I'm not only a professional—as a mother of three boys, I know how wonderful and challenging parenthood is, and I want other parents and children to benefit from OT the way my family and I have.

Sometimes, in the heat of the moment, it's easy to forget that problem behaviors have reasons behind them—they aren't skin-deep. Once the root of the behavior is understood, the underlying problem may be addressed. But when your child is sitting down in a supermarket or parking lot crying hysterically, or standing quietly on the sidelines at a school fair behind an invisible wall, it's hard to remember: *These and other challenging behaviors may be your child's way of coping with his inability to fully register sensory input, or a result of stress on an unbalanced nervous system.*

Rather than seeing your child's behavior as antagonistic, think of it as a mystery to be solved. A child's behavior gives us clues into how he lives life, how he operates, and how he adapts to the world. Stress can keep him from adapting. Stress is usually made up of a combination of environmental and internal stimuli. For example, blaring sirens (environmental) combined with a child's sensitivity to noise (internal) may produce stress. Or, your child might have a hard time coping with multiple forms of simultaneous environmental information, combined with the inability to tune out distractions and pay attention. Of course, there are many other types of external and internal stimuli that might be stressing your child's systems as well.

On a basic level, the work I do helps children's nervous systems deal with stress. By using occupational therapy interventions, I help children develop the skills they need for daily living, helping them feel more comfortable in their own bodies. Occupational therapy helps minimize dysfunctions that cause behavioral issues, and often leads to improvement in the child's schooling and social life. It gives children a better quality of life, allowing them and their parents to be more satisfied and happier. For example, helping children become calmer, yet at the same time focused and alert, enables them to react less to distractions, and therefore, pay more attention in class. In many cases, I've helped children gain the ability to "roll with the punches" and adapt to environmental fluctuations; then, situations that once stressed them out are less of a problem (or not a problem at all).

I want children to be happy, productive, motivated, and able to live life fully, applying their beliefs and values. The therapy I do helps them achieve this. But the truth is, it usually takes hard work. There are two approaches to helping children with challenges function more effectively in this world. One approach says, *Adapt the world [the child's environment] to meet the child's needs.* My approach is: *Give the child the skills and know-how he needs in order to adapt to the world.*

One of my patients is now a fifteen-year-old boy. His teacher signed him up for an elective that he is not interested in, instead of the elective he wanted. He went to the teacher and asked her to make a switch. She refused. He came home and told his mom. She spoke to me about this and told me she was going to confront the teacher, who, admittedly, appeared to be inflexible.

I suggested she not get involved. "Josh is fifteen years old. He will have to learn how to deal with all kinds of people and situations, and he is certainly old enough to start now. If you step in for him now, will you be prepared to step in for him when he's dealing with a stubborn boss?"

Every parent wants to help and protect their child. But sometimes kids have to learn how to deal with even unpleasant situations. Dealing with the world as it is can make kids stronger and give them important skills, such as the ability to negotiate. Allowing them to live in the world as it is can also help them develop capacities for acceptance, resourcefulness, and resilience. My goal is to help children (and their parents) develop the skills they need to achieve more meaningful and satisfying lives. This is about self-actualization.

When I see a child who was once anxious now appear calmer, happier, and more focused, I celebrate. When I see a child who was once rigid and inflexible adapt to meet new challenges, I know I've achieved my goal. Brianna was formerly in the special resource room, but is now doing "fabulously," says her mother. In fact, she just got a 100 percent on a recent test. Of course, the goal isn't necessarily getting perfect scores (although that's always nice!), but developing the ability to focus, stay calm, and feel centered enough to learn in a classroom setting is a big achievement for a girl like Brianna.

Where there's a child who is improving, there's usually a more confident parent who is enjoying his or her child more. I also measure success by how much better the parents are doing, too. I know I've made a difference when a mom or dad tells me, "Before, when my child had a meltdown, I had a kind of meltdown, too. Now, even though the meltdowns are far less frequent, if my child does have one, I feel in control." Most parents understand that the OT was partly for them, too. In fact, the entire family benefits. And I feel there is no work I'd rather be doing—it's my mission.

But I can only help so many children and parents on a one-to-one basis. That's why in the last few years I've also begun to teach parents, educators, and other professionals. In my lectures and workshops, I help the audience see their children, students, or clients in a new light. I want them to understand that the disruptive child in their homeroom, or that "slow" child in their English class, is probably experiencing the world differently from their peers. This difference may cause anxiety, difficulty concentrating, problems interacting with teachers and classmates, and other issues. Even the most well-intentioned teacher or professional (or parent) might feel that disruptions are purposeful when they often are not. It's especially important for teachers to realize that a child with behavioral and learning issues may be exceptionally bright and talented, but caring and effort need to occur in order for them to detect what the underlying issue is. Then, they'll be able to turn on this child's shining light.

I believe, however, that lecturing and doing workshops isn't enough. Children are in school only part of the day, and parents may not have the time to attend talks and workshops. I knew it was extremely important to reach more parents directly, which is why I decided to write this book.

The first part of my book is a guide to helping your child. To keep it simple, I chose to address some of the most frequent problems kids have, problems I see in my practice all the time. I offer solutions for four major problems, which I identify as follows:

1. Child-on-the-Edge: This is the child who is reactive, rigid, and stressed. Any discomfort or change can set him off. Tantrums, rigidity, and hysteria ensue. This can be painful, embarrassing, and uncomfortable, as well as highly stressful for parents. Very often the parents and kids butt heads.

2. The Princess and the Pea: This is the child for whom the slightest unpleasant sensation is exquisite torture. A tag on the back of a T-shirt, a windy day, the ticking of a clock—the child experiences sensory input as painful and highly distracting. He or she may cry, withdraw, or become anxious.

3. The Heat-Seeking Missile: This is the child who needs highly-stimulating activity, the more rambunctious the better. He seems to thrive on disruptive or downright dangerous situations. With him, your heart is always in your throat.

4. The Squeaky Wheel: This is the child who lets you know what's on her mind. Always. She will complain and cajole until you give up and give in. Talk, talk, talk.

These are issues that can be partially addressed by parents at home, with an accessible, do-it-yourself approach, using some techniques from my practice as an occupational therapist.

The activities in this book are OT techniques, a scientific, yet creative blend. These include unique exercises, practices, and lessons, which I call "interventions." These interventions might be as complex and subtle as methodical emotional work, or as simple as applying deep pressure to the shoulders. You can use the interventions alone or to supplement the work your child is doing with other professionals, including occupational therapists. Of course, I recommend you speak with your child's therapist about using these interventions, but overall, I believe in trusting your heart. Your good parenting instincts are natural and can be relied upon if you're in touch with them.

The interventions in this book are designed to help your child feel more comfortable with who he is, and give him a measure of self-awareness and confidence. They will help him manage and regulate his feelings, emotions, sensations, and behaviors. They will help him navigate the complexities of his environment without becoming overwhelmed.

Some of these interventions are also a lot of fun and can be approached as play. Because you will be spending time with your child doing something you both enjoy, your relationship will grow stronger. You will understand your child better and find interactions with him to be less intense. Any one-on-one quality time between parent and child is beneficial; I believe these interventions are special not only because the activity is an effective clinical technique, but also because while doing the activity with your child, you will be focusing on him, giving him the attention he craves. Sometimes even a moment or two is all that's necessary to help your child regulate himself and become calm and focused.

As you do the interventions (and get any other support you or your child may need), your child's ability to regulate his emotions and behavior will begin to improve. As you progress, you'll find you've helped your child learn how to self-regulate—this skill will have grown much easier for him. Then, both of you will feel less frustrated.

As you get to know and understand your child in a new way, you'll be able to predict potentially challenging situations and help him prepare for them. Of course, there'll be times when you'll need to handle unpredictable situations; then you'll have the opportunity to use new tools to help you deal with them. You'll learn the skills you need to support your child as new or challenging situations occur. As you become more attuned to your child and begin to more deeply understand and become aware of his needs, you'll find that your relationship will become stronger and healthier. You'll also find that you and your child will be more "in sync." You'll understand that his behaviors are usually cues that express a need, rather than being "bad" or simply "disruptive." You'll be able to recognize and respond appropriately—you'll become an expert at interpretation! You'll know when he really needs your attention and when he doesn't. Soon, both of you will feel more in sync.

But, helping your child isn't enough. You need to help yourself. Becoming more aware of who *you* are and what *your* needs are can actually help your child (and, of course, it's important for your sake, too). Socrates said, "Know thyself." It is, indeed, important to know what helps you stay calm and centered, and which situations can potentially trigger uncomfortable feelings. While no one can learn how to avoid every uncomfortable situation (nor would we want to), we can learn how to manage our emotional responses to even unpleasant experiences. We all have moments (or days), where stress after stress piles up, and we feel out of control.

That's why Chapter Six of this book shows you how to help stop the stress cycle, and also gives you tools for change. It won't be news to you that behavior issues can lead to a kind of "tape loop" of disruptive or frustrating behavior: frustrating behavior leads to anxious mommy or daddy who responds negatively, which leads to more disruptive or frustrating behavior, and an even more anxious mommy, until the whole day feels like a disaster. The use of simple tools, though, can help both you and your child regain balance.

Don't let the simplicity of the language or interventions fool you—these are excellent techniques for helping your child regulate his behavior, as well as for helping you do more than cope. The interventions are easy to do and engaging. You don't need a background in science or psychology or occupational therapy to do them. But, I want you to understand a bit more about what causes these behaviors at a whole-body level, so the first chapter explains what a child's healthy, regulated system looks like, how a child with a dysregulated system experiences the world, and how stress occurs and leads to challenging behaviors.

I also want you to know that you can contact me and ask me questions regarding the content of this book via email. So, instead of tucking my email way in the back of this book in small print, here it is: TheParent-ChildDance@OTThrive.com.

Chapter One: The Stressed Child

Sometimes what appears to us—parents, teachers, and other adults—as "bad" behavior, may be a child's way of trying to cope with bodily or emotional stress. In order to understand what a stressed or *dysregulated* child experiences, we have to understand how a non-stressed child goes about his day. A non-stressed or *regulated* child likes both quiet play and noisy play, each in their own time and place. A regulated child can enjoy the stimulation of rough and tumble play, and afterwards, can re-center himself and go about his day, either on his own or with the help of a parent who is in tune with his needs.

A regulated child, often with the help of a parent, is able to withstand some periods of low-activity and can amuse himself, in ways that aren't destructive or harmful. He can handle changes in routine, sometimes with a little reassurance from a parent, and can acclimate himself to being around other trustworthy adults and children who don't belong to his immediate family. A regulated child isn't rigid. Sure, he might, on occasion, be stubborn—he'll sometimes ignore what his parents ask him to do if it's a task he finds unpleasant—but usually, he's flexible enough to handle ups and downs, successes and disappointments. He can sit calmly in class at least much of the time, and is able to focus on lessons. Allowing for differences in personality and predilections, a regulated child is generally content to be in whatever environment he finds himself in presently, with reasonable exceptions.

This does not mean perfection. A child of nearly any age, who had his heart set on going to the circus and is now told he'll be spending the afternoon with Great Aunt Gertrude in her nursing home, will be disappointed. He might complain, cry, scream, or otherwise fuss. Even a regulated child who excels in sports might find sitting in a classroom for nearly seven hours a day stressful and uncomfortable, and will likely find the last hour or two of school difficult to endure. A regulated child who is able to spend hours amusing himself drawing an intricate picture, may find, however, that going on a long, muddy hike is unpleasant and stressful. But overall, a regulated child is able to function, have satisfying relationships with his parents, siblings, teachers, and friends; be productive; have fun; and adapt to and enjoy life's variety.

A stressed or dysregulated child is one who experiences discomfort much of the time. His state of discomfort makes his world hard to adapt to. He might overreact or shut down. He may appear distracted, withdrawn, insatiable, angry, sad, rigid, clumsy, overly-particular, whiny, or confused. He may have what I call a "mind-freeze," during which he can't be reasoned with. He's responding to the stressful sensations he experiences in the only way he knows how.

When you think of stress, you may think of environmental stimuli such as traffic, an argument with your spouse, rushing for an appointment—these are stressors that can affect your emotions and your body. You might also think of toxic fumes, loud noise—for instance, New Year's Eve at Time's Square in New York would be a stressful place to be for many. Or, food could be a source of stress (such as peanuts or gluten if you have a particular sensitivity them). Food especially may affect your body first, and then affect how you feel emotionally. All these stressors can have an impact on how you or your child function.

Some children (and adults), are more sensitive to what's going on in their environment than others. Events that most children would regard as mild might affect the bodies and minds of certain other children profoundly. On the other hand, some children seek out experiences that most of us would consider stressful; their bodies and minds get stressed when the environment isn't "exciting" or dynamic enough for their systems to process—loud drumming, roughhousing, and trampoline are what they crave. And some children struggle with stimuli that aren't even environmental, they are primarily internal—their systems are constantly being stressed by internal messages. For example, they are always hungry because they rarely feel full no matter how much they eat. This causes them to be whiny and maybe even overly-chatty. These are children who are often, or even always, in a state of dysregulation.

Please note, I recommend that if a child isn't functioning optimally, even if he is already being treated by an occupational therapist, check with a nutritionist in order to make sure he is getting the proper vitamins and minerals he needs, and that the foods he's eating are agreeing with him. I often refer my clients to nutritionist Kelly Dorfman, author of a terrific book called *Cure Your Child with Food: The hidden connection between nutrition and childhood ailments* (Workman, 2013).

In order to really understand how your child responds and reacts to the world around him, we'll need to understand that the first point of interaction between world and self is the sensory system. Hearing, tasting, smelling, touching, and seeing are the most well-known senses. When your quiet-loving child hears a very sudden loud noise, for example, the information goes to his brain, which immediately signals that there is a potential danger: his heart may start to beat faster, his blood pressure may rise, his ears may turn red, and, most noticeably, his pupils may dilate and his breathing may become shallow. While these physical responses are symptoms of stress, the symptoms themselves may also trigger feelings of anxiety, contributing to an escalating cycle of tension. Soothing music might calm the quiet-loving child, while hearing other children playing outside will distract him, and he'll find it difficult to concentrate on homework or other activities.

When a child tastes something bitter, pungent or smelly, such as garlic or fish, he might react by spitting out the offending substance or even gagging. Sometimes, on days when you wash the floor with a scented cleaner, your child may find the smell overwhelming and have to leave the room. But after a while, his sensory system may "tune out" or "tell" the brain to stop responding to a non-threatening, though unpleasant, odor.

When a toddler strokes a fuzzy blanket or an infant is swaddled, they usually become calmer. Touch has two subsets. The first kind, *superficial touch* is tactile, like the fuzzy blanket example. If you lightly rub your fingertips over the page of this book or reading device, for instance, you will experience the tactile sense of touch. Often, a light touch on the skin can be irritating for children; it can feel like a spider is crawling on them. Now, press strongly on your forearm with your palm. What you are experiencing is a deeper kind of touch, from your proprioceptive system, the kind of sense a swaddled infant feels. The deeper receptors beneath your skin in the muscles, joints, and tendons are being activated. Often this kind of touch is very calming for children and even adults.

What your child sees can also be a powerful sensory experience for them. Nearly ninety percent of our sensory input comes from sight. We instinctively know this when we shield our child from viewing media that is violent or otherwise inappropriate for his age level. We all know that color and light have an impact on our moods, as does a beautiful view or a painting. For some children, a view out a window or door can be distracting while sitting in a classroom.

There are other senses in our system, too, one of which is the vestibular sense, which is related to how the body moves and experiences movement. There are two sub-types of vestibular senses. One type is how the body and head experience sensation together, and the other is the head alone. Vestibular input contributes to the sense of balance, head control, muscle tone, visual perception, how well eyes work together as a team, and level of alertness. For example, your teenager might enjoy a roller coaster ride or snowboarding. Your older child or toddler might enjoy swinging, jumping on a pogo stick, or riding a bike or scooter. An infant needs to be rocked.

To experience your vestibular senses try this: As you are sitting down, bend your neck so your head moves up and down several times, as much as you can tolerate. Now, stand up and bend and straighten your knees, moving your entire body up and down. The first activity illustrates the more intense sensation associated with the head's vestibular movement sense. The second illustrates the less intense sensation associated with the vestibular movement sense of the entire body (including the head).

With all of the senses, your child is constantly interacting with and being influenced by the environment. For some children, it feels as if the environment is bombarding them. If their sensory system is overly responsive, the sensations they experience will cause them discomfort. As a typical child develops, his brain learns which stimuli to pay attention to and which to ignore. His brain will automatically filter out information that he does not need to pay attention to. A dysregulated child isn't able to do this.

In general, the ability of each child's brain and body to modulate or control how he senses the environment is unique. Your child may be more sensitive to some stimuli than others, or less or more sensitive overall. A child's ability to effectively utilize sensory information is fundamental to how he functions—in school, at home, and with friends and peers.

There's Too Much Input: I Need Less

Your child might be extremely sensitive to stimuli, and he might find it uncomfortable, threatening, or painful. If so, his sensory awareness is set on "overload." Children who are hyper-sensitive respond to the unpleasant sensations they experience by avoidance, aggression, or other coping mechanisms. Thus, the little girl who may appear to be painfully shy in large groups may be feeling very uncomfortable from all the motion or noise. The baby who stiffens up when caressed may find the touch too light and therefore irritating. The little boy who hits, kicks, or screams at other children may be experiencing their physical closeness, even a friendly hand on the shoulder, as uncomfortable or threatening. After-school meltdowns may be frequent, as transitions, such as that from school to home, can be overwhelming for the sensitive child.

A sensitive child may try to gain a measure of control and insist on doing things "my way or the highway." He may feel vulnerable or exposed and refuse to wear short-sleeved shirts, or chew on his clothing or other objects. What we see on the surface—withdrawing, shy behavior, disinterest in affectionate play or touch, rigidity, or aggression—are actually messages the child is sending us, if only we know how to interpret them and how to help.

Admittedly, it can be confusing. Different children exhibit similar behaviors for different reasons. The boy who pushes, hits, or yells might be saying, "Hey, you're giving my brain way too much information—I'm overloaded and I can't cope."

Or, he might be saying, "I need more sensory input!"

There's Too Little Input: I Need More

Or, he might be telling us something different: "I don't know where my body is right now, so I'm going to do something intense to my body so that I can feel where my body is. This will help me feel safe and stable." This child may be hypo-sensitive to the world around him. He feels deprived, even starved of sensation. He needs more movement or noise or other stimuli in order to feel something.

A toddler who spins around and around may be generating stimulation for himself. A five-year-old girl who talks incessantly, or constantly plays on her pogo stick, may also be attempting to satisfy her need for stimulation. A six-year-old boy who loves to bang on pots and pans, screams at the top of his lungs, and pushes his siblings or engages in very rough play may feel more satisfied with these more aggressive activities than when he plays a game like softball, or sits in a classroom. He is attempting to self-regulate, and trying to adjust his arousal level so he can be comfortable. A child may feel frustrated or anxious to the extreme if he isn't able to get the level of stimulation he needs. It may even feel like "life or death" to him. Some under-stimulated children express themselves overly dramatically, as if to say: *I'll die if I don't get what I want.*

Virtually all children (and adults, too), are more sensitive to some stimuli, and less sensitive to others. But this doesn't always lead to dysfunction. A child can function reasonably well if he can't tolerate loud music. A child can function well if he needs to run and jump a bit more than some other children. But, when the hypo- or hyper-sensitivity leads to problems at home, such as an increasing number or intensity of tantrums, or lack of meaningful interaction with the rest of the family, this is the level that meets the definition of dysfunction. If the sensitivity leads to the inability to stay calm and focus in class, this, too, is dysfunctional. If a child has difficulty making friends because he's either withdrawn or overbearing and aggressive, this can also be problematic. The interventions in this book can help a child regulate his sensory experience so that his awareness of sensation begins to move toward a more acceptable and comfortable level for him.

Why do some children have sensory systems that do not function as well as others? In some cases it might be genetic. Sensitivities, like other aspects of personality, can run in families. It might also be congenital, which means hyper-sensitivity begins in the womb. Also, a premature infant might be born with a nervous system (which includes the sensory system) that hadn't finished fully developing. Poor diet may also be a contributing factor. Trauma in a child's life can also be a significant factor. Environmental toxins in the air, water, or home such as pesticides and chemicals in household cleansers, also may contribute to the poor functioning of the body's systems. We know that even an adult who experiences a trauma, such as abuse, being a victim of crime, or living through a war, may have a variety of symptoms and/or posttraumatic stress disorder. But, whatever the reason, occupational therapy (OT) can help.

My practice, Thrive Occupational Therapy, is founded on the belief that a child's whole system is involved in healing, not just the brain or body. Also, family dynamics, culture, and spiritual beliefs are all part and parcel of what helps a child and family heal. A person's cognitive, sensory, physical, developmental, psychological, and spiritual functions all work together holistically. While it's true that sometimes treatment may need to focus on one aspect of an individual's system, all the other aspects are always involved, whether we have awareness of this or not.

The activities I chose to include in this book are intended to support the healing of the entire person. You may use the OT interventions in this book in conjunction with occupational therapy, but you may also use them to supplement or support other kinds of healing modalities, including psychotherapy, physical therapy, nutritional or medical treatment, and spiritual practice. Because my approach is holistic, I find that employing some techniques, which might be considered psychological, social, developmental, and spiritual, during OT sessions, makes treatment more effective.

I describe four very common behavior types in this book in the next four chapters. However, as you read, you may notice that your child seems to "fit" into more than one chapter. That's okay, there is plenty of overlap and having one set of challenges doesn't preclude a child from having others. The truth is, I chose these types of behavior categories in order to make it a bit simpler for you, the reader, to choose activities and interventions that can help *your* child, but absolutely *not* to pigeonhole or label your child.

Finally, before you move on to the other chapters in this book, I'd like to say a word or two about mindfulness. Chi-Kwan Shea and Robyn Wu have a beautiful definition of mindfulness, especially as applies to occupational therapy, which is published in *OT Practice*, the official journal of the American Occupational Therapy Association:

Mindfulness is the ability to increase one's attention to the present environment as well as to self, which may include one's emotional states, bodily sensations, and cognition, in a non-judgmental and accepting manner.

Although the goal of the interventions in this book might sound complex, in actuality, the objective of each of them is to help achieve mindfulness. When you and your child become more aware of how he is experiencing the world, you can both find ways in which to make that experience more comfortable, productive, and meaningful.

Chapter Two: Child-on-the-Edge

I ntensity!

The "Child-on-the-Edge" feels, experiences, talks, and acts with such intensity that other people—including even loving parents—can feel overwhelmed in his presence. Words and phrases that might be used when referring to your on-the-edge child include the following:

- Tantrum
- Over-reactive
- Hyper-sensitive
- Easily frustrated
- Nervous Tics
- Talkative

- Anxious or Nervous
- Shaking or Spinning
- Whirling Tornado
- Wild
- Radiating Energy
- Bright and Quick

And of course, Intense!

Is your child a Child-on-the-Edge, who might be helped by the interventions in this chapter? If you are able to easily and frequently apply the above terms to describe him, he likely is a Child-on-the-Edge.

It's important to keep in mind that each child is unique, and may or may not exhibit every single characteristic trait associated with the Child-on-the-Edge (or the other behavior categories named in this book). I want to remind you that the only reason I've identified these categories is to make it easy for parents to find the interventions best suited for each child's challenges. If your child's a Child-on-the-Edge, he probably exhibits many of the attributes listed above, much of the time. But again, don't be surprised if his behaviors or attributes overlap with other chapters in this book, especially the Heat-Seeking-Missile child described in chapter four.

Another way to tell if your child is a Child-on-the-Edge is your response to him. Are you drained by his energy? Do you feel that you are walking on a tightrope, never sure if you'll be able to maintain control of your emotions or the situation? Do you find yourself longing for peace and quiet? Do you dread non-school days? Do you worry that you rarely seem to simply enjoy spending time with your child?

Throughout this book, I describe children with behavioral challenges who were helped by specific interventions I implemented as part of a larger course of treatment. I've shown these parents how to do these interventions at home, and I explain how to do them in this book. It's important to note that these interventions, when performed as described, help many children regulate their systems and gain a new sense of calmness, focus, and well-being. The interventions can be used alone, and you will notice some improvement, and in some cases, a lot of improvement. Still, in many cases, these interventions are most successful when used to enhance and support a more comprehensive course of occupational and/ or other therapy. It's also good to remember that most children will enjoy participating in most of the interventions in this book and that any child, even one who only occasionally experiences self-regulation issues, can benefit from them. In fact, although I highlight specific core issues each intervention can help with, they can be applied more broadly. You may want to experiment with several or even all the interventions in this book.

•••

Calvin was a bright six-year-old, whose mom was often exhausted by his intensity. When Calvin entered a room, you sensed it—his energy was palpable. He was hyper-aware, very talkative, and insisted on doing things his way. Bedtime was arduous; he had difficulty falling and staying asleep. He was very sensitive to any kind of touch. He "overreacted" to minor distractions and would easily "melt down." He went from zero to sixty in the blink of an eye. He was also aggressive and provocative with children his own age, and most interactions with his peers seemed to end in fights and arguments. Joyce, Calvin's mom, felt he might have ADHD, though he was never formally tested or diagnosed. When I asked her to tell me the most difficult time of day for Calvin, she answered, "*All* the time." In other words, Calvin was a Child-on-the-Edge.

I explained to Joyce that Calvin craved a higher level of sensory and emotional input. He needed to "feel" more. This is why he'd provoke other kids—he wanted them to respond and give him that input. However, because he was emotionally sensitive as well as sensitive to touch, he would become angry and overwhelmed, despite the fact that he unknowingly invited this aggressive attention. He'd then tell his teachers and parents that he'd been bullied. Once embroiled in a confrontation, other children were unable to sense when Calvin had had enough, and they would continue to roughhouse, leaving Calvin feeling overloaded and overwhelmed.

To calm himself, Calvin would rock and sometimes bang his head. He'd also squeeze and hug his siblings very hard, another way of getting the input he craved. Because Calvin didn't have a good sense of where his body was in relation to his environment, he craved a lot of movement, which helped him sense his body. Overall, his coordination was poor and his movements were often awkward, jerky, or rigid.

One of the first things I wanted to do was to help Calvin move his body in a more fluid, responsive manner. After a few months of using the interventions I include here as part of a larger course of treatment, we saw measurable improvements in this area and others.

Calvin's body was mostly in extension, with locked elbows and knees. A child such as Calvin, who has difficulty going from flexion to extension and vice versa, is believed to have an unintegrated *Moro reflex*, which is very common in many dysregulated children, including the ones I write about in this book. The Moro reflex is normally present in infants and newborns. It is a reflexive action that occurs when an infant's head drops backwards and he has the sensation of the head not being supported, he responds with extension. That is, he inhales and spreads out his arms and legs.

After extension, the baby should recover by returning to flexion: he'll exhale and pull his arms and legs in toward the middle of his body, recovering into a loose fetal position. In regulated children, the Moro reflex is usually integrated by four months. This means that when the nervous system is stimulated, and the body is alerted, it is able to recover fully in a reasonable amount of time. The Moro reflex is not the only reflex—there are numerous others that help a child regulate, but descriptions of them are beyond the scope of this book.

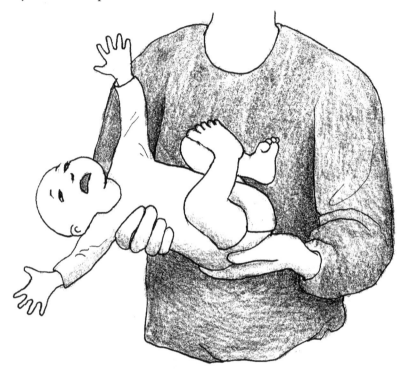

Moro Reflex

The flexion position "protects" a person from too much input. The extension position, however, exposes the body to a lot more input, because more of the body, including more vulnerable parts of the body, are exposed. When in the extension position, our bodies present a wider target.

Imagine a chunk of cheese. A block of cheese has six sides and comparatively less surface area than that same block sliced into several slices. Those thin slices expose more surface area of the cheese. The slices of cheese are more prone to mold and spoilage, are able to be more easily squashed—in other words, they are more vulnerable to assaults on their material integrity. The child whose Moro reflex is not integrated experiences a startle response more frequently because more of him is wide-open to the world without the natural, self-protective boundaries others have. This child may walk on his tiptoes with back arched. Also, knees and elbows may be locked and there may be stiffness in their feet.

I wanted to help Calvin to develop his healthy, flexion middle-ground. I also wanted to help strengthen Calvin's inner core—the muscular system, including the diaphragm, which helps us breathe, as well as stabilize the trunk and pelvis. When we say someone is "centered," we are painting a verbal image of a person with a strong inner core—which is, after all, the very center of the body. A person who has a strong center is able to focus and attend and doesn't get overly silly.

A child whose inner core isn't as strong as it could be is a child who has a hard time recovering from various types of stressful input. He is less able to regulate his feelings and emotions. He has difficulty calming down when upset. He might even get "stuck" in a feeling, such as nonsensical silliness. This is the child who can't stop laughing once he gets started; the child who might even fall and get hurt when he's feeling "silly" because he is overly excited. He can't manage to find his center and get back to a calm state. Having a weak inner core also affects the movement of the eyes and reading, as these are dependent in part on healthy breathing, the primary function of the inner core musculature.

•••

Pop Goes Your Child!

The first intervention I recommend is one that addresses Calvin's weak Moro reflex and weak inner core. It's easy to do at home. It is based on the work of occupational therapist Sheila Frick. I call this activity "Pop Goes 'Calvin!'" (use your child's name in place of Calvin's).

1. Your child lies on his side on the floor in a loose fetal position, making sure the soles of his feet are pressed firmly against a wall. Gently help him tuck his chin down into his chest, as much as is comfortable for him.

2. In a clear voice, count down: 10, 9, 8, 7, 6, 5, 4, 3, 2, 1…POP! When you say "pop" your child pushes his feet off from the wall, extending his hands up and above his head, and zooms away from the wall in a fast, fluid motion. He may end up on his stomach or remain on his side—allow his body to go in a direction that feels natural to him.

3. Since one side of his body will have received tactile input in the form of deep pressure, I like to have children go "Pop!" again, this time on the opposite side of his body.

4. Now have him try a third time, this time on his back, his knees bent toward his chest, his feet flat on the wall in front of him, his chin slightly tucked down to his chest.

5. Finally, if he's comfortable on his stomach, he can do it face down, his forehead resting gently on the carpet or his head turned to one side, his knees tucked under him. Remember to help him keep his chin slightly tucked.

6. Repeat at least three to five times on each side.

7. Variation: Make it a contest. You and your child do "Pop! goes…" together, measuring whose feet get farther from the wall—the one whose feet are farther away wins the round!

Special Equipment: None.

Pointers: At first, you might want to demonstrate this for your child when you are in a room together. Even if you don't explicitly ask him to watch you, he'll probably be intrigued and ask what you are doing. He may even volunteer to try it himself. When your child is doing the intervention, you can count down alone or he may count down with you. Make sure he is resting completely on the side of the body he is going to be sliding on. When he is on his side, his arms and legs should both be in front of him and tucked into a real fetal position. Your child might find a wood floor, bed, or other surface more comfortable than carpet. Siblings, cousins, or friends could also have a contest to see who gets farther.

Pop Goes Your Child! Step 1

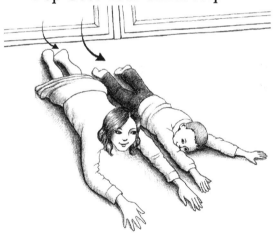

Pop Goes Your Child! Step 2

Balloon Blowing

This intervention, based on the work of Mary Massery, PT, DPT, DSc, strengthens the child's inner core and steadies his breathing. It is an intervention I especially like to teach to occupational therapy students when I lecture. As a guest lecturer in Dr. Mary Falzarano's occupational therapy class at Kean University, I've frequently received positive feedback on this intervention.

Dr. Falzarano has influenced my thinking on the importance of mindfulness. This intervention focuses on the breath, which helps with mindfulness (attention and focus, too), as well as the ability to calm down and recover from upset. It also strengthens the ability to deal with anxiety and stress and, like all exercise that involves taking slow, deep breaths, is immediately relaxing!

1. Your child is given balloons to blow and begins to blow one. He stands facing away from you.
2. Squat down behind your child if he's small; otherwise, stand behind him. Place both of your hands on his last few ribs on either side of his rib cage. Your child will take a slow exhale into the balloon in order to blow it up.
3. As he does so, press in firmly on his ribcage, using the palms of both your hands (not your fingertips).
4. When he pauses from blowing and takes a breath in, release your hands so they rest lightly on his rib cage.
5. Repeat several times until he's blown up a couple of balloons, if possible.

Special Equipment: Balloons

Pointers: Make sure your hands are not on the soft part of your child's belly nor under the armpits, only on the last few ribs. Do not press so firmly that it is painful. Gently coach your child to take slow, deep breaths out, in order to blow air into the balloon. Some children may have difficulty coordinating in-breaths and out-breaths. If so, go slowly or demonstrate how to do it. Buy good-quality balloons. It's a good idea to practice first on yourself or on another adult so that you can understand what this activity feels like.

Balloon Blowing

•••

Pizza Massage

Pizza Massage is a popular, calming, and fun type of massage, with a high level of interaction between parent and child. I borrowed this known activity from another treatment modality—massage therapy! For all those kids like my brother, who always wanted to own a pizza shop—this is an activity they'll love!

1. Have your child lie face down on the floor.
2. Tell your child that first, "we make the dough." Make a fist with both hands and using the flat part of the back of your fingers (not the knuckles) knead the back gently, starting at the shoulder, on either side of the spine. Then, gently knead the arms and legs, and include the soles of the feet if your child likes the sensation.

17

3. Tell your child "Now, we spread the sauce." I say we "shmear" the sauce—children love silly-sounding words. Using the flat palms of both your hands, firmly but not too hard, press down and as in Step 2, go down the back, up the arms, and down the legs and feet. Again, making contact with all the areas is more important than going up and down; you might prefer going around and around.

4. Now, "we'll put on the cheese." Holding your hands in a "karate chop" position, use a firm (but not too hard) chopping motion all over the body, as in Steps 2 and 3.

Special Equipment: None.

Pointers: You can do any of the three types of massage for as long as your child likes in whichever area of the body feels best to him. Children have individual preferences about what feels good to them and these preferences might even change from day to day. You may vary the intensity of the massage by varying the speed and pressure. If your child is allergic to pizza or doesn't like it, you can rename the massage, calling it the "bread baker's massage," the "sandwich maker's massage," "the salad mixer's massage," or whatever type of food is appealing to your child.

•••

I taught Calvin's mom how to read the clues to his behavior. A child's behavior reveals what he needs and which sensory systems might need more sensory information or less. In my practice, I show moms and dads how to be behavior-detectives so they can become their child's external regulators. Then, they are able to teach their children to notice what their own actions and reactions mean. For example, when Calvin would squash the baby, Joyce would say, "It seems that maybe you would like to be squished? How about a pizza massage, or I can help you squish your body under couch pillows?" By expressing this aloud, a parent will eventually help their child become more aware of his needs and how to meet them.

•••

Hannah was an adorable, hug-loving four-year-old with big, brown eyes. Her parents were both busy doctors, who scheduled time each day to engage in Hannah's and her siblings' education. Hannah appeared anxious when she first came to see me in my office—her fingers played around her mouth and sometimes her belly button. Like Calvin, Hannah had a very hard time sleeping; she'd grind and clench her teeth. She also transitioned poorly from one activity or environment to another.

Mary, Hannah's mother, told me Hannah was moody and often had tantrums or cried easily—crowds, unexpected noise or movement, or even seeing a new person could "set her off." Often Mary, as well as Hannah's older brothers, would give in to Hannah's tantrums and allow the four-year-old to get her way. They'd do this in order to avoid conflict, which was sure to erupt if they didn't give in. The tantrums and crying made Mary feel anxious; in fact, Mary told me she, herself, had anxiety.

I explained to Mary that Hannah exhibited signs of emotional and sensory dysregulation and that there were interventions that may help her respond to sensations in a more balanced manner. Hannah's inability to stay calm was related to the fact that she used only some of her core muscles while breathing. Hannah needed to strengthen both her inner core (breathing and stabilization muscles in her trunk and pelvis, see the section on "Calvin" earlier in this chapter), and her outer core—the muscles in the abdominal area that we use for movement. Within a few intensive sessions, Hannah's tantrums had improved slightly; after a few months, the tantrums were of markedly shorter duration, became much less intense, and happened only once or twice a month, rather than a few times a day.

The first intervention I used with Hannah is called *Nok 'Em Down 'N' Roll 'Em*. It helps children strengthen their inner core and improve the quality of their breathing. Like many children with weak inner cores, Hannah breathed mostly with her belly in shallow, rapid breaths. This intervention helped her breath more deeply using all the breathing muscles of the trunk of her body. It also strengthened Hannah's hand-eye coordination. For Hannah and most children, this activity is a lot of fun.

•••

Nok 'Em Down 'N' Roll 'Em

Nok 'Em Down 'N' Roll 'Em helps children strengthen their inner core and their eye-hand coordination.

1. Line up at least ten toys, a couple of inches from the edge of a table. These should include two or three plastic dolls or other figures. You may also include three or four small or medium toy cars. Matchbox size or smaller works best.
2. Have your child sit in a chair, or stand, facing the toys, and give her a good-quality, old-fashioned party blower. Ask her to use her breath and the blower to knock down the doll figures and roll the cars across the table. Gently guide your child's blower toward the toy at first, if she seems to need help making contact.

Special Equipment: Table and chair. They can be child-sized or a regular kitchen table, as long as the toys are somewhere between eye and shoulder level. She may have to bend over slightly—that is fine. Toys and party blowers (have a few extra on hand in case one breaks). I suggest you use good-quality party blowers because I've found that the cheaper ones only work once.

Pointers: This is an intervention that most kids love, but be sure to choose appropriate toys. Lightweight toys are easier to blow or roll than heavy toys. Wider or bigger toys that provide more surface area are easier for your child to target. You do not have to use a table and chair; you can even do this on the floor while kneeling. You can do this intervention several times in a row if your child enjoys it.

Nok 'Em Down 'N' Roll 'Em
• • •

Hat Trick

Hat Trick is based on Rogue Dumbo, an intervention created by Anthony T. DeBenedet and Lawrence Cohen in their new classic, *The Art of Roughhousing*. I taught Hannah's mom this intervention to help Hannah get into the flexion position, because she had a tendency to want to be in extension rather than flexion, just like Calvin. Hat Trick will give your child plenty of calming sensory input, as well as spinning and energetic fun.

1. Stand and lift your child into a big hug, wrap your arms around her, and have her wrap her arms around your neck or upper back and her legs around your torso. Support her bottom with one hand and place your other arm around her back or neck.

2. Hug her tight and, in broad movements, rock side to side or back and forth, while counting aloud to ten, singing a favorite song or nursery rhyme (for example, the ABCs).

3. Then say, "Okay, here goes…" Little by little, let go of your child's upper back, making sure her legs are still wrapped around your body, and help her let go with her arms.

4. Then, encourage her to slowly bend her head and torso down and backwards (upside down), and extend her arms down and out. She should be hanging onto you with her legs. You should be supporting her by her thighs and/or lower back.

5. Swing around and around, and ask, "What's the trick?" (or use any phrase or make any sound that will make it even more exciting for your child.)

6. Stop and say, "Hat Trick!" and you child will stretch down and reach for a hat that you've placed on the floor.

7. Now, encourage her to pull upward using the strength of her stomach muscles and arms, and ask her to place the hat on your head.

8. Then, have her return to the hugging position, while her hands are clasped firmly together until she is once more in the original hugging position.

9. Repeat.

Special Equipment: One or more hats and a good, strong back!

Pointers: If you have a colorful bunch of silly or interesting hats, your child will enjoy choosing between them. Many children love the feeling of freedom spinning brings, but it can be scary for some to "let go" and hang upside down or backwards. If your back is not strong, you don't have to spin or even let her fall backwards. Just hold your child, sitting or standing, and have her give you a big hug with her arms and legs wrapped around you, for eight to ten seconds. If she likes the feeling, hug her back. Then, release the grip—repeat the hugs three to seven times. Some children respond to being hugged (firmly or loosely) by becoming calm; others find it irritating. Some enjoy the spinning; some do not. Play this one by ear.

Hat Trick Step 1   **Hat Trick Step 6**

• • •

Hannah had a hard time acclimating to new situations, such as large parties and gatherings. Therefore, I suggested to her mom that she prepare her in advance by doing the following: Using Hanna's favorite stuffed animals, dolls, or mini-people, create a scenario of the upcoming event. Act it out with the toys, then have Hannah act it out. This way, Hannah knew what to expect. Each year I get an update from Hannah's mom, who tells me that Hannah is making good adjustments from one grade to the next, and is enjoying her friends and family, even at busy, loud parties, which used to be overwhelming.

• • •

Sam, an exceptionally bright six-year-old child is a "big thinker." According to his parents, he had high levels of anxiety much of the time, which is why they brought him to see me. I could see that sometimes Sam clenched his teeth, drawing his arms and shoulders tightly together. His entire body also shook, indicating that he, indeed, was trying to release anxiety and tension. He also exhibited nervous tics, which the teacher said had become far worse when he began to learn how to read.

His parents explained that Sam's anxiety appeared to be triggered by changes in routine, even slight ones. Also, when he was hungry or tired, or if someone hurt him, he would react strongly, shaking and hugging himself. Sadly, other children, especially his siblings, usually reacted in a negative manner to Sam, belittling and teasing him. This was extremely painful for him.

Sam's parents told me he frequently enjoyed spinning around, indicating that his body needed more input to feel itself in space. This helped him regulate his system. It gave him input he craved. I recommended an intervention that he would love to do, one that is easy and fun, called *Spinning in a Chair*.

•••

Spinning in a Chair

After Spinning in a Chair, which will give your child the stimulation he needs, he will most likely feel calmer and more focused, as long as the spinning is rhythmic enough and repeated enough times. He'll have to reach his own threshold, which is different for each child. Some kids need additional structure when doing this intervention. If so, try having him spin in time to a simple, rhythmic song, a metronome, or your own count.

1. Position One is sitting—this is the least intense. Position Two is lying on the side in fetal position, chin tucked, hands under the head to keep the spine in alignment with the head—this is medium-intense. (He can also flip over to the other side, as well.) Position Three is lying on back, knees bent into chest (make sure back of head is resting on a chair)—this is medium-strong intense. Position

Four is lying on back with legs bent over or wrapped around the back of the chair and head hanging upside down off the chair—this is the most intense position.

2. Start with your child in position one. Spin the chair, asking the child how fast or slow he likes to go. Repeat, trying each position if your child wants to. Leave it to your child to choose the position and speed, and the number of spins. However, start with only one or two spins—this kind of input can be very powerful.

3. When you're done, spin in the opposite direction, clockwise or counterclockwise, for the same number of spins. This helps balance the inner ear.

Special Equipment: Office chair that can spin, a spinning board, or a large lazy Susan, but not a Sit N' Spin™. Virco makes good quality chairs.

Pointers: Increasing speed increases the intensity; allow your child to choose how fast to go. At first, carefully monitor how many spins you do. Start with fewer spins—rotary input is powerful. Start with the least intense position, allowing your child to decide if he wants a more "exciting ride." If so, move up one position in intensity. Some children feel more comfortable if they are holding weights or have a slightly heavy object such as a blanket or pillow on top of them. You can repeat the intervention a few times if your child enjoys it. Repeat until you feel your child has had enough or if you see him begin to exhibit *any* signs of stress reactions, such as pale skin; red ears; sweating; short, shallow breath; or nausea. Sing a rhythmic song, count, or use a metronome to add structure to the activity.

A reminder: As with any intervention in this book, do not overdo it.

Important note: If you or your child gets dizzy, here are some ideas to help: Stop, have him sit upright, and press down firmly on his head with your palm. He can also take a sip of water or breathe in some cool air. Some children love spinning, others dislike it intensely—use your judgment.

Spinning in a Chair Position 2

Spinning in a Chair Position 4

•••

Intensity Fix

I created this intervention to help children like Sam, who may need to feel strong pressure on their bodies in order to feel calmer.

1. If your child is angry or tense and his fists are clenched, that's okay—it's the perfect time to tell him you're going to do Intensity Fix.

2. Slide and press: Press *down* firmly on his shoulders, sliding all the way down to his hands, grasping them firmly and sliding off them. Repeat three to five times.

3. Firm press: Now, press *in* firmly on the sides of both shoulders simultaneously, then press *down* simultaneously (and firmly) on his upper shoulders, then continue on with the sides of his torso, then his hips.

4. Repeat the action in Step 2, the sliding-press motion.

Special Equipment*:* None.

Pointers: Don't give your child verbal directions such as "calm down" or "relax." The firm pressure alone will help him release tension. You might try pressing firmly but gently down on top of your child's head, too, if he likes. Acknowledge how he's feeling. (See Chapter Six, under In-Sync).

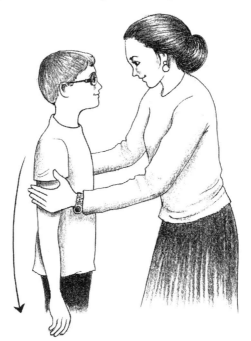

Intensity Fix

•••

Sam's mom explained to me that she often didn't know what set him off into his clenched-teeth-raised-eyebrows-hands-clenched mode. I asked her to use my *Breathe, Look, Assess* technique instead of reacting immediately, as his siblings were doing when they made fun of him.

Here's how to do Breathe, Look, Assess: Take a deep breath and wait a moment while observing your child. Think about what he is reacting to and why. Once you think you may have an idea, you can say to him, "I see you're very frustrated about _____." You may even say this while you are doing the Intensity Fix.

If you don't have an idea of what's going on, ask your child for his input. You might say, "I'm not sure what's going on; can you tell me if something is bothering you?" As you speak to your child, it's important to show plenty of facial affect so the child senses that you are in tune with his feelings. (See Chapter Six, under "Attunement Parameters.")

Chapter Three: The "Princess and the Pea" Child

Overwhelmed!

Like the fairytale princess, your Princess- (or Prince-) and-the-Pea child could probably feel a pea through a pile of mattresses. The Princess-and-the-Pea child wades through a swamp of overwhelming sensations every day. Every sound, taste, smell, texture, light, color, or other sensation is experienced with a heightened sensitivity. Many Princess-and-the-Pea children constantly monitor what their sensory experiences are and how it makes them feel—and they feel compelled to share these feelings with parents, siblings, or others. Sometimes the Princess-and-the-Pea child can make parents feel like saying, "Enough already! It's only a breeze (a name tag, yogurt, a bit of garlic, a ticking clock, a fluorescent light…)."

Words and phrases that might be used when referring to your nothing-more-than-feelings child include the following:

- Hyper-sensitive
- Overly-sensitive
- Raw
- Pained
- Picky
- Unaffectionate
- Needy
- Avoidant
- Fearful
- Anxious
- Squirmy
- Over-emotional
- Frustrated
- Chatty
- Overly-expressive
- Tearful

And of course, Overwhelmed!

To your Princess-and-the-Pea child, the world is an annoying, uncomfortable, or even painful place. This child is unable to filter or integrate sen-

29

sations, which is why they are said to have poor sensory processing. Sounds, sights, tastes, smells, and textures don't fade into the background—to the Princess, each individual sensation feels like it is constantly clamoring for attention. This can be overwhelming; this child might do his best to avoid the disturbing feelings, so much so, that they withdraw.

The flickering light that mildly annoys you might irritate your Prince or Princess to the point of extreme frustration. The smell of garlic or fabric softener can be so overwhelming that the Princess-and-the-Pea child gags—or even vomits. Some tastes, textures, or temperatures of foods or drinks might also trigger this reaction. It might take your child a few weeks to get used to a new T-shirt or a change from short sleeves to long—the weight, color, and texture are different, and the transition is a challenge. Most of us find a pebble or sand in a shoe annoying; for a Princess-and-the-Pea child, a tiny irregularity in a sock or a label on a T-shirt feels like a boulder or sandpaper!

Many of these children are also extremely sensitive to various sounds—the hum of a refrigerator, traffic, certain musical instruments, or even musical notes may be actually painful to their ears. And a sudden noise, even a soft one, can startle. Other sensations, such as motion, can also cause discomfort for your Princess-and-the-Pea child. Travelling in a car might be difficult—motion sickness may occur on even short trips. An amusement park ride (even a merry-go-round), might be out of the question. Even any unusual physical position, especially when the head is not in alignment with the body, may cause this child to become dizzy or uncomfortable.

A trip to a concert, sporting event, party, or the mall seems like a trip to a battlefield to this child. Noise, jostling, high-pitched voices, and other sounds are all simply "too much." If you think back to the last time you were stuck in major traffic or had to attend a very noisy party after a long day, and magnify how stressed this made you by ten times, that will give you some idea how your Prince or Princess feels.

You probably find that your Princess-and-the-Pea child needs to be soothed and comforted more often—these children might even do self-soothing and self-comforting actions, such as chewing on ice, sucking on objects, hugging themselves, wrapping themselves up in a soft blanket or towel, covering their ears with their hands, lying down in a dark, quiet room, genital rubbing, and so on. They might even need sunglasses on a cloudy day.

This chapter features two girls with poor sensory integration (a teenager and an eight-year-old girl), as well as Tyler, an eight-year-old boy. Arielle, a seventeen-year-old client of mine, tells us in her own words what it feels like to live with poor sensory integration.

•••

Arielle

I'm 17 and have extremely poor sensory integration. Until a year and a half ago, I didn't realize that the suffering I experience is due to sensory defensiveness. You may be blessed with a life free of the pain I endure on a daily basis and you may wonder how it would feel to be me. Let me attempt to describe my life to you.

I live my life in a thunderstorm. Every small disturbance that I experience is magnified ten-fold.

To me, simply sitting outdoors feels like a run in a downpour—it's sensory bombardment. We could both be relaxing in the shade, me and you, but have vastly different experiences. You see, my senses perceive things exaggeratedly and sitting in the shade can feel as uncomfortable to me as a run in a thunderstorm feels to you.

The cool breeze that you enjoy brushes the hair against my face again and again, irritating my skin. It feels like raindrops. The emergence of the sun from behind a cloud is a bolt of lightning to me. The aftertaste of my morning poppy-seed bagel lingers on my breath. You innocently flip the page in the novel you read, and the sound scares me like a howling wind. A gnat brushing against my cheek feels to me as startling as a black cat darting in front of you. It disorients me and I accidentally tip some lemonade onto my lap. The napkin turns my skin a cherry pink as I attempt to wipe the spill. The smell of lemon lingering in the air tickles my nose and I gasp for a clean breath of air. I reach my hand down to itch the area of skin irritated by the napkin. You look up from your book, relaxed and refreshed, and announce that you are ready to go. "How about a trip to the mall?" you suggest. You look surprised to hear that I need to unwind first. But I just had a run in a thunderstorm.

I suffer from a full range of symptoms affecting all my five senses. Here are just a few examples: Until I was twelve, I was only able to wear cotton clothes. I can only sleep with three pillows, arranged just so. I get a migraine from the smell of cheese, garlic, and pizza.

I am [always] on high alert. I notice a chair tilting backward before it crashes. A low whistle or high-pitched tone of voice is a piercing shriek. A fluorescent light bulb is as bad as a flickering light. A twisted sock feels like a twisted leg and I lose the ability to concentrate on anything else. I need double the personal space of an average adult—don't come too close! I cut my nails twice a week. My food can only be eaten at medium temperature. A ball thrown in my direction in a game of catch feels like a bull is charging towards me. (It's a fight-or-flight situation in which I choose flight.)

I cannot sit still for more than 30 seconds. That's seven hours of fidgeting on a regular school day. Using playground equipment is equivalent to riding a roller coaster. The ups and downs of a slide can do that to me. To top it all off, it takes me two hours to complete the transition between school and home.

With occupational therapy, my life has gone from being an unrelenting thunderstorm to a light and manageable drizzle. There were many exercises that I feel helped me tremendously, but one stands out in my mind. With the help of Miriam, I constructed a therapeutic swing made of elastic materials. I swing in it for approximately an hour a week. In the swing, I finally feel calm; the elasticity hugs my body and relaxes me.

Listening to therapeutic music has helped me overcome my sensitive hearing. For nearly a year, I listened to therapeutic CDs with specialized headphones for half an hour, twice a day. It took a lot of discipline to keep to the rigorous schedule, but the effort paid off. Thank G-d, I can now say that I am ninety percent free of my sensitivity to sounds.

•••

These exercises, and the interventions I've included in this chapter, helped reorient Arielle by exposing her to sensory stimulation in a safe environment. Arielle ends by telling us, "I feel taller and I don't need to nosh like I usually would. I feel energized, I feel large, like big. I feel really grounded and steady. I hope to continue working with my OT until even the fog lifts off." In addition, we met her goals of becoming calmer and not so hyper-alert, not being afraid of touch, feeling happier, and thinking about dating in the future.

The first intervention is called Ice Cream Cone, which helps strengthen breathing. Children who are tense and anxious nearly always have trouble taking full, measured breaths. However, this is an extremely important factor in regulating the body's systems. But full, measured breaths are important—the Princess-and-the-Pea child is usually tense.

•••

Ice Cream Cone

Ice Cream Cone strengthens breathing and breath control, especially the exhalation. There are numerous versions of this activity used by both speech- and occupational therapists; you can get creative and come up with your own version.

1. Place assorted "magic" growing capsules or sponge shapes (such as animals, cars, geometric shapes, and so on), in a plastic basin or pail. Add a few squirts of gentle, non-toxic dish liquid or hand soap, and fill with water from the faucet, stirring with your hand to make a lot of bubbles. Set the basin down on a low table or chair. The surface of the table should be around chest level.

2. Your child will take a plastic straw and put one end in the water, the other in her mouth, and blow out, into the water, in order to make the maximum amount of bubbles. Tell her she's making an

ice cream cone—the bubbles mound and look like ice cream on a cone. You can join her with your own straw, demonstrating how to blow long, slow breaths down into the water, not short bursts of breath.

3. After a big mound of bubbles is made, ask her to reach down into the water, take out a foam shape, squeeze it out and guess what it is. She can do this with or without looking at the shape.

Special Equipment: Plastic basin or a pail. Assorted sponge shapes, in the shape of animals or people (you can cut these out yourself or buy them). Liquid dish or hand soap. Room-temperature or slightly warm water. Plastic straws, or tubing from a refrigerator or air conditioner, about one inch in diameter.

Pointers: If your child has a latex allergy, be sure that the equipment you are using is latex-free. You can alternate Ice Cream Cone with the Balloon-Blowing intervention or Nok 'Em Down 'N' Roll 'Em.

●●●

Tactile Box: Version One

This activity is good to do before the next version, because it acts as a warm-up to help children get used to touching various textures, especially if they are sensitive to texture.

Assemble items in a plastic storage box or other type of box or bag. Possible items to include: a piece of fur, a sponge, a bumpy toy, a stress-relieving ball, a washcloth, a piece of silk, sandpaper, assorted brushes (hair, paint, nail, etc.), a dish scrubber, a ball of yarn, etc.

1. Have your child close her eyes, or cover the box with a blanket or towel, and ask her to reach in and choose an object. Have her feel the object with her hands and try to identify it. Have her continue as long as her attention is held.

2. Alternately, you may place some objects on a table in front of your child and ask her to keep her eyes closed, then feel and identify the objects.

3. In another version of Tactile Box (there are many), have two of each object. Make two piles, being sure each object's match is in the other pile. Have your child close her eyes and ask her to match each item to its mate. Have the child look at the items first, if she is not familiar with them.

Special Equipment*: Plastic box or other type of box or bag. As-sorted objects, see above.

Pointers: You may choose to do Tactile Box with various fabrics only, or three-dimensional objects only (related or not), to help the child develop finer sensitivity. You should update the box from time to time. Your child may wear a blindfold if she likes or you can buy an inexpensive pair of sunglasses and put stickers on the inside of the lens.

•••

Tactile Box: Version Two

This version is done daily, over a period of two months, or until im-provement with sensitivity to textures and touch is achieved.

1. Assemble items in a plastic storage box or other type of box or bag. Possible items to include: a piece of fur; a sponge; a small, bumpy ball; a stress-relieving ball; a washcloth; a piece of silk; sandpaper; assorted brushes (hair, paint, nail, etc.); a dish scrubber; a ball of yarn; etc.

2. Each day, choose at least two items with different textures. Rub items, one at a time, over child's back, arms, legs, and, if tolerated, the belly, face, and neck, including under the chin. In Arielle's case, she rubbed the items on herself. Your child might like to try that, too.

3. Start with textures and areas of the body that are least sensitive to your child. For example, some children who can't tolerate a wash-cloth find rough items like sandpaper pleasurable. The three most sensitive areas are generally the face, the belly, and the bottom of the feet.

Special Equipment: Plastic box or other type of box or bag. Assorted objects.

Pointers: Generally, children prefer you rub them in the direction in which their bodily hair grows. If your child has eating or speech issues, try to rub items on and around the mouth. When you notice that your child is not as sensitive to touch and textures, when she is able to tolerate a T-shirt tag, pajamas, underwear, being touched suddenly, and so on, you can cut back to using the Tactile Box a few times a week, and eventually taper off.

•••

Hand Hugs and Stretch

Neurodevelopmental therapist Janet McDonald finds much benefit in massage-based exercises like Hand Hugs and Stretch. She says, "If you check, you'll find that massage has been used on the planet since ancient times. The practice of manual compression and assisted compression has been used therapeutically since man began attending to his own and others' maladies. Also, Dr. Tiffany Fields, of Touch Research Institute at the University of Miami, has done much research into a variety of touches like the ones in this activity." Hand hugs are done with gently-cupped palms, applying even pressure from all directions. Hand Hugs are done on the arms and legs.

1. Cup your palms so that they both fit snugly, but gently around the limb you are working with at the time. Your fingers may be interlaced or overlapping. Give firm, but gentle and loving "hugs." Squeeze gently around in at least three or four places on the forearm. Begin at the fingers, hand, or wrist, depending on your child's preference, and hold each position for eight to fifteen seconds. Instead of holding to a second count, you can try giving hand hugs with your child's natural exhalation, then release, and put your hands in the next position while your child inhales. Repeat in a comfortably slow rhythm. When you get to elbow and shoulder

joints, be sure that your hand hugs remain gentle—the joint areas in the arms and legs may be sensitive.

2. When doing the leg, start at the toes, feet, or ankle, depending on your child's preference, and continue on until just before the upper thigh. You may place one hand beneath the part of the leg you are working on, and one on top. When you get to the pelvis area, place one hand beneath the joint (at the hip) and the other above. Be sure not to press too hard. Avoid the inner thigh. Make sure that your hugs on the joints, especially the ankle and knee, are not too firm.

3. Repeat on the other side of body.

4. For the stretch: Hold your hand above and below each joint. Start with the fingers or wrist (depending on your child's preference) and move on to the elbow, shoulder; then, toes, or ankle (depending on your child's preference), knee, and hip joint. With a gentle grasp, use your body weight to apply a stretch by pulling gently on either side of the joint for eight to fifteen seconds.

5. When stretching the legs: Hold above the ankle and the foot, and gently stretch with curved, not flat palms. When doing the knee, hold above and below the knee and stretch gently to activate the stretch in the knee joint. Gently grasp the outside of the hip joint with one hand, and grasp the ankle with the other, then slowly stretch, in a smooth, motion.

Hand Hugs And Stretch Step 1

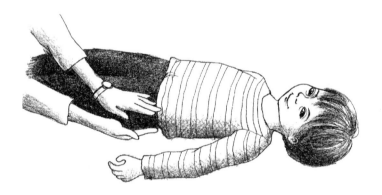

Hand Hugs And Stretch Step 2

Hand Hugs And Stretch Step 4

Special Equipment: None.

Pointers: Firm, but gentle pressure is best for the Hand Hugs. Use your palms and finger pads, not your fingertips. Pull *gently* as you stretch—this stretch should be done in a smooth movement. Let your child's response be your guide—if he likes the stretch, then continue; if he's very uncomfortable, stop. If he's enjoying some sections of this intervention, then linger a bit longer.

• • •

Because Arielle was a college student, I did the emotional work directly with her, not with her parents. I made sure to point out when she seemed less sensitive, more jovial, and more conversational. I also was sure to give her positive feedback whenever she followed through on her OT homework. I regularly asked her for her feedback so that together, we could evaluate what was working for her, and what wasn't.

• • •

Tyler was brought to see me when he was eight years old. Like Arielle, he was sensitive to noises, textures, and other input. He was afraid to blow his nose and didn't like the feeling of getting wet, so bath time was a real hassle for his mom. Tyler was bedwetting nearly every night and exhibited many signs of anxiety. Although his Mom was a successful high-achiever, she was anxious due to a lot of external pressures. Tyler may have sensed his mother's anxiety, and this appeared to compound his own.

Tyler was a constant chatterer (more about this type of behavior in Chapter Five: "The Squeaky Wheel"). He had a hard time playing ball games, difficulty with handwriting, an immature pencil grasp, and poor manual dexterity in general. He also had problems with eye tracking, which exacerbated his manual dexterity issues.

Tyler was coping with an unintegrated Moro reflex issue, as well as poor balance and general clumsiness. In school he was fearful if playtime involved balancing games. He was in a state of constant alert—he walked on his toes, eyes wide open, eyebrows up. He always fidgeted with his hands and he held his back arched. His body was like a satellite dish—open to signals at all times. I wanted to help him develop a more neutral, or even protective stance, so that he didn't constantly feel bombarded by input from the environment.

The tactile-defensive Princess-and-the-Pea reacts to sensory input with alarm, angst, even panic. Sometimes tactile-defensiveness is the primary root of more functional problems and dysregulation, as in the case of Arielle. But sometimes, nervous-system dysregulation is only one part of the problem. In Tyler's case, emotional issues were an important factor. Although trauma of some kind might be a contributing factor in some cases, this was not so for Tyler.

However, the constant state of his and his mother's high anxiety added to Tyler's difficulties. Tyler's situation is not unusual—to varying degrees, there are often both functional and related emotional issues in tactile-defensiveness and other sensory integration disorders. Although treating the emotional issues is important, it's good to start with techniques from occupational therapy, many of which have been suggested in this book and which can help stabilize some of the nervous system issues first.

Within eight months of treating Tyler with a variety of interventions both at my program and at home with mom, Tyler showed dramatic improvement. His anxiety markedly diminished. He only occasionally walks on his toes. His handwriting has improved and, as of today, is well on its way to being at grade-level. School has improved for him overall, and he's made some really nice friends. Recently his mother reported that he eats more neatly, has better balance, and no longer wets the bed.

••••

Figure Eights

Figure Eights, or The Infinity Walk, was developed in the 1980s by psychologist Deborah Sunbeck and is widely used in a variety of disciplines, including occupational therapy. It benefits overall coordination as well as head, neck, and eye coordination and also helps with posture and balance. The first version is relaxing and both versions are easy to do at home.

1. In this easy version, which assists in relaxation, the child stands bent over at the waist, arms hanging. With a loose, swinging motion, he moves his upper body and arms in a figure eight over and over again. He can stop when he feels dizzy or when it's time to move on to another activity.

2. In this version, two objects, such as kitchen chairs, or two piles of two or more pillows, are set up facing each other (in a row) about four to five feet apart. About midpoint, outside of the path of the chairs, is a marker—an object the child will focus his eyes on. You may choose to be that object of his focus, or you may choose a painting, flashcards, a video, or picture album, etc. Have your child walk a figure eight, looping around the chairs at the top and bottom of the eight. He should be focusing his eyes on you or the object at all times. He should not look at the floor, the wall, or the

path he is walking, but the object only. Over time, this helps him strengthen his coordination.

3. Now, your child can try moving along the figure eight going forward and backward.

4. Now, he can try moving along the figure eight while crawling, forward and backward, all the while, still only focusing on the object.

Special Equipment: Two objects, such as kitchen chairs or two piles of pillows, to mark the spots. Pillows are great because if the child bumps into them, they're soft. But chairs are easier to notice with peripheral vision. Use whatever works best for you and your child, or come up with another marker.

Pointers: You can demonstrate each version for your child. You may also want to initially walk the figure eight with your child, in which case, designate an inanimate object as the marker. Use your imagination: Your child can hop on one foot, jump, skip, or find another way to move through the figure eight.

Figure Eights Step 2

• • •

Rocking Horse

This intervention helped Tyler move into the flexion—or more protected position. Over time, he stopped toe-walking and arching his back and eyebrows, and began to walk in a more neutral manner. This intervention is loosely based on Child's Pose.

1. Your child lies on his back, knees pulled into his chest, hands holding right below his kneecaps. His neck and head are off the ground, looking toward his knees. His torso is curled up toward his knees, which will happen almost automatically if he is lifting his head toward his knees.

2. He rocks for the count of ten side to side. An alternate version is head to toe, if he prefers.

3. He then stretches his arms above his head, with both head and legs on the floor for the count of three.

4. Repeat Step 2.

Special Equipment: None.

Pointers: You may support your child's neck and head to start, if he finds this difficult. Count out loud, quickly enough so the momentum from each rocking motion carries the child back and forth. Allow your child to do several rocking motions in a row. Try to keep a consistent rhythm. This activity may be done a few minutes each day.

•••

Just as Tyler needed the world around him to be "perfect" in order for him to feel comfortable (not too noisy, nothing surprising, only certain textures and foods, and so on), he also felt the need to *do* everything perfectly himself. This increased his anxiety. Imagine, for example, if you always felt compelled to look perfectly put together at all times—this would naturally cause you anxiety.

What I did, and what I encouraged Tyler's mom to do, was to compliment him when he did things *imperfectly*, saying things like, "I like the way that drawing you did didn't come out exactly as you wanted it. Yet, you were still okay with it."

Or, "I like the way you left the picture half-finished. And, that you were so easy going about how it looked."

Giving positive attention and praise is something you can do to mold your child. You can even create moments to help him easily succeed with a character trait he's not generally strong in, such as being positive, flexible, or responsible. I adapted the following technique from Howard Glasser's Nurtured Heart Approach. Mr. Glasser calls this "hijacking" the moment.

You give positive attention to your child when he is exhibiting a character trait you want him to strengthen—even if you have to create the moment. For example, it might be a treat for your child to be given the car key and told he can go out ahead of you and unlock the car doors with it. Within a few seconds, follow him, and give him recognition for being so responsible with the key. Because this is fun and novel for him, and because you are giving him only a few seconds before you come out and acknowledge his positive choice, you've created an event at which he can succeed in an area that is usually challenging for him, in this case, being responsible.

Chapter Four: The Heat-Seeking Missile

Energy!

The Heat-Seeking-Missile child can swerve from one physical activity to the next. When it comes to emotions, he can do zero to sixty in a few seconds. He needs to be on the move—sitting at a school desk is torture for him. Words and phrases that might be used when referring to your Heat-Seeking Missile include:

- In-Motion
- Jump
- Run
- Twitch
- Squirm
- Tantrum
- Wild
- Screaming and Yelling
- Crash
- Knock
- Bump

- Crunch
- Noisy
- Spin
- Risk-taker!
- Hyper
- Overdrive
- Rigid
- Novelty-seeker
- Impulsive
- Me First!

And of course, Energy!

•••

The Heat-Seeking Missile and the Child-on-the-Edge from Chapter Two often overlap. However, the Heat-Seeking-Missile child needs and craves the stimulation of extreme sensory input, especially motion, whereas the Child-on-the-Edge is agitated and unnerved by many kinds of sensory input (although he might also crave other kinds). For the Child-on-the-Edge, even subtle sensations cause anxiety. If you are seeking a better understanding of your child or some activities that can help your child, don't be concerned about overlap, just choose the interventions that seem like a good fit for you and your child.

One of the things I learned from my mentor and friend, occupational therapist Kimberly Barthel, is that you can learn so much from doing an intervention with a child even if it isn't overtly successful and doesn't get the "results" you'd like to see. By paying attention to how the child participates in the intervention, you may pick up clues about your child you wouldn't have noticed otherwise. Also, it's important to remember that change may be subtle—it's likely to be small and incremental.

The alert and vivacious Heat-Seeking Missile is constantly active, but though he may be athletic, some of these children are also clumsy and uncoordinated. They might crave speed, but lack control—this is the child who'll ride his bike down a giant hill then skid and crash—sometimes on purpose. These children can be fearless when it comes to speed and danger!

A Heat-Seeking Missile longs for the thrill of the chase, and the excitement of new adventures, but can have problems transitioning to activities he isn't in the mood for. He also may be quite rigid about getting his own way and may have little empathy for others, more from an inability to get outside his own immediate and pressing needs than any innate lack of kindness. Like a missile, he has a target, and it can be difficult to stop his trajectory.

The Heat-Seeking Missile child is, in old-fashioned parlance, a "handful." He is the child that simply can't sit still and finds close-focus games and books—and often being in a classroom—practically unbearable. If your child's a Heat-seeking Missile, he might not respond to you when you ask him something or call his name—again, it's because he's intensely focused on something and everything else seems far away or irrelevant. Of course, this can be frustrating for a parent—especially if your child answers you rudely when he finally is able to shift his attention.

•••

Ethan, one of five children, came to Thrive OT when he was four years old. His mother told me she didn't know where to turn—Ethan jumped on people, even strangers. He constantly put both food and non-food items in his mouth, didn't sleep much, and never seemed to have any down-time. He would awaken a few times each night and scream—really loudly. Then he'd pop up and go to his parents' bedroom. His behaviors only seemed to intensify as he got older.

When Ethan decided to do something, he embodied the missile—he'd do whatever it is without asking permission or caring what anyone else's concerns were. He only answered to his name about twenty-five percent of the time and rarely responded to verbal instructions. He became explosively frustrated when he was restrained from doing what he wanted. Although Ethan was able to dress himself, he preferred his mother to do it. He didn't like to sit in a chair—he'd get up or fall out. This prompted his mother to feed him while he was lying down or sitting. Because he was usually on the go, she often had to chase after him, desperate for the chance to get some nutrition into him.

Both his parents were concerned for his safety—Ethan was fearless in the playground, jumping from very high places. He also used playground equipment in new, and often dangerous, ways. He really was without fear; if provoked by other children, he'd fight back, kicking and hitting, even if they were a lot bigger and older. He also seemed to not feel pain—he'd somersault into the family's stone fireplace and appeared to be unaware of his scrapes and bruises.

Ethan would get bumped up from clumsiness, too. He sometimes fell down the stairs, and he easily tripped over objects or his own feet. His balance was poor and he had a poor sense of direction and little awareness of himself in space.

During our first visit, I could see that he was alert to sensation, but he wasn't always able to process, or make sense of, what his body and senses were experiencing and feeling. This made self-regulation a big challenge for Ethan. After evaluating him, I was able to see that his proprioceptive system was under-processing sensory information. It was also hard for Ethan's sensory systems to prioritize experiences. This is why Ethan and some other Heat-Seeking Missiles appear "clumsy" and don't seem to hear you when you call them.

Note: *It's important to first make sure to have a doctor check your child's hearing and vision, if he doesn't respond to you.*

How does a child like Ethan feel?

Imagine that you are on a diet. You are cutting back from three huge meals a day plus limitless chocolate milkshakes and other high-calorie foods to a small breakfast, lunch, and dinner. You wake up and have an egg-white omelet and a small apple. Ten minutes later, you are starving. An hour later, you can't focus on anything but food. Finally, at lunchtime, you decide to cheat, and because you've been so hungry all morning, you eat two sandwiches, a large order of fries, and a giant piece of cheesecake (and of course, a diet soda). You must gorge in order to feel satisfied.

A child like Ethan is just as starved for sensory input as the extreme dieter is for food. He keeps seeking stimulation and finds ways to create it, such as pushing, shoving, and so on. He goes into overdrive in order to satisfy his need for sensation. He'll keep going until he feels satiated—and that might take hours, an entire day, or longer.

At school, Ethan was impulsive, touching the belongings of other children and even the teacher. He was oblivious to what was going on in the classroom; he'd jump up and erase the board while the teacher was talking. He'd bite his clothes and other objects, jump around and touch other children. This disrupted the class, especially during circle time.

Obviously, his parents found Ethan's behavior frustrating, even painful, and they asked me if I could help them. Because Heat-Seeking Missiles generally respond well to occupational therapy, I said the likelihood was high that their son would benefit from treatment. I worked with Ethan and his mom for nine months, during which time, he made quite a turnaround, both at home and in school.

At the end of nine months, he was able to sit in a chair throughout an entire meal, was more grounded, and less likely to injure himself. Although he still occasionally had bouts of wild behavior, most of the time he listened and responded to correction, and was able to better regulate his feelings and behavior. He also rarely had tantrums anymore when he needed to transition from what he was doing to something else. Overall, he was calmer, and so were his family members and teachers.

An important part of what we did was to educate his teachers and the school administration about Ethan's difficulties. I created some pointers for a game plan they could use so Ethan could perform his best. Then his mother and I did plenty of interventions, both at home and in my office.

When he transitioned into kindergarten, his teachers were very pleased with his performance. He was able to sit at his desk and focus. He participated in all subjects, and began making healthy friendships. He spent play time interacting with other children, not just roughhousing. He was even able to sit and play sedentary games.

Ethan's parents received only one call about misbehavior that entire school year—a far cry from the previous year, when Ethan's behavior was the main focus of parent-teacher conferences. They were proud parents, indeed, when his teachers told them at a PTA meeting how delightful a child he was.

•••

Blow the House Down

Blow the House Down is a preventive intervention. It's comprised of three breathing activities, which result in calmness, yet are exciting enough to hold a kid's interest. They'll help your child develop better breathing techniques and strengthen the breathing muscles.

The breathing the child learns and practices while doing these interventions is clinically proven to help kids calm down faster from a tantrum. But it's important to remember: Use these interventions preventively—don't do them while the child is having a tantrum. There's a bonus, too:

once your child is able to calm his emotions down, then you'll be able to use your parenting skills more effectively.

I have found the children I work with in my practice, calm down far more quickly from tantrums *100 percent of the time* when they practice better breathing. When a child uses all his breathing muscles daily, you'll see dramatic results.

You can do all or some of the following activities. Trying spreading them out over the course of a day or week, as time permits. (They require inexpensive gadgets, easily purchased online.)

1. Citra Citrus Sipper™ is a special straw. Poke the sharper end into an orange and hand it to your child. He'll probably know what to do! Your child will suck up the delicious juice, swallow, and breathe. This cycle helps kids become calm and centered and is good before they sit in a classroom, during lunchtime, and right before homework. This also develops oral muscle strength.

2. Blow String Pipes is a pipe with a colorful string attached. Your child will blow into the pipe, watching as the string bobs up and twirls with his breath. This captivating intervention works on breathing, blowing, and helping your child stay calm and focused. It also helps his eyes with tracking, which will improve his reading skills and help his eyes work together more effectively as a unit. It also doesn't make loud noises as most whistles do.

3. Blow Pens are colorful airbrush pens powered by your child's breath! Your child can use the stencils that come with some blow pen kits, or use them in a coloring book, or to decorate a poster for his bedroom (maybe post it on his ceiling for a treat). You can ask him to draw a self-portrait, or let him decide how he wishes to use them. This is great for breathing, blowing, and eye tracking, and will help your child become calmer and more centered.

Special Equipment: You can purchase a Citra Sipper, for use in the first intervention, online. I got mine at floridabymail.com. The special blow string pipe is available at dysphagiaplus.com and other online suppliers. A variety of blow pens, blow pen kits, and stencils are marketed online under the name Sprayza™. They come in many variations for different ages. They are made by melissaanddoug.com.

Pointers: If your child is allergic to citrus, do not use a Citra Sipper. The child can massage and squeeze the orange all over in order to release more juice. Citra Sipper is a great idea for snack time in school, as it'll help him focus and attend during the next part of the day.

The Blow String Pipe, which comes in packs of three, is easy to carry with you on trips, as is the Citra Sipper. The blow pens are a fun activity to do along with your child during bonding and connection time, especially if you use a large piece of butcher paper. This allows for more freedom of movement and expression. You can tack a large piece from a roll of white easel paper to the floor to keep your child engaged for a while (you'll want to use an old blanket or flannel sheet as a drop cloth). You can buy or make your own stencils, or your child can draw freely.

Note: If you or your child blow too long, you might become light-headed.

•••

Climbing and Crashing Plus Squashy Sandwich

This intervention can be done while your child is "wild"—it will help put structure into rough and rowdy play, and will eventually calm things down.

Ethan didn't like spinning, but he loved fast, thrilling activities. Climbing and Crashing helped him feel and release explosively intense energy. Squashy Sandwich, which we did right after Climbing and Crashing, helped him get the deep pressure his body craved and integrated his proprioceptive system. There's an added bonus to doing these interventions: these activities are FUN. Plus, parents can get in their own work-out, too. Finally, Missile children love the high level of engagement—Mom or Dad is finally joining them in an activity that they like, instead of something "boring" that requires sitting still.

1. Your child climbs a sturdy object—maybe a sofa, a strong table, a jungle gym, etc.

2. Then, he jumps off and crashes onto a soft landing space, such as a mattress or crash pad, or a bunch of couch pillows.

3. Holding a bean bag, sofa cushion, or similar pillow, lie (not too heavily) on top of the child when he lands. The cushion should be between the two of you so that a wide area of pressure is applied to the child's body, anywhere from the shoulders down.

4. Say, "The sandwich is in the toaster, but it's not quite ready yet" as you apply the pressure with the cushion (but not too hard; remember, you weigh a lot more than your child). Make sure your child can breathe easily—he'll probably also be laughing, as this is loads of fun for him. Or, he'll be grunting to get out from under you before you can "eat him up."

Special Equipment: A sofa or table; mattress or crash pad (you may need more than one); sofa seat cushions; and large, firm pillows from a chair or bean bags.

Pointers: Make sure the object your child is climbing is sturdy. Make sure the space is clear, except for the object and the crash pad. If necessary, you can divide this into two separate events. Crash and Climb is one, Squashy Sandwich is another, although they do work together well. Using a sequence while playing helps calm things down. In this sequence: climb, crash, squash, climb, crash, squash, and so on. I suggest you finish with a *squash*. If your child becomes overly excited during this or other movement activities, try one of the other blowing activities in this book first, such as Blow the House Down.

●●●

In Ethan's case, I went to his school to speak with his teachers, assistants, and principals. Here are some of the ideas I gave them: There are different areas that can help calm a child like Ethan. They are the relationship, the breathing, and the sensory system. (You can do the following at home, too.)

For the relationship: Do some gleaming and beaming. Give the child a happy smile with your mouth *and* eyes—even from across the room. This lets him know when he is behaving appropriately without the need for you to be close up or to speak.

For the breathing: Face the child and breathe deeply and encourage him verbally to do the same. Or give the class a blowing activity to do.

For the sensory system: Give the child two pieces of frozen gum or ice cubes. This will often help a child center and calm down; he won't need to mouth other objects. It also strengthens oral musculature.

For the auditory system: Form a cup or tunnel with your hands around your mouth so they create a megaphone effect. Speak through the "megaphone" in order to direct your voice toward the child and help him focus on what you're saying.

•••

Eight-year-old **Julie** was an amazing gymnast—a bright, popular girl who wore a high ponytail and attracted friends with her vivacious personality. She was also a Heat-Seeking Missile. Her mother described her as being on "overdrive" from the moment she woke up, and said that she rarely stopped talking. Julie was able to hold it together in school, but often had a meltdown when she came home, the place where she could "let go." She would hijack the conversation, talking nonstop. She'd take control of any situation and rigidly demand her own way (she always wanted a particular seat in the car, for instance). She was quite bossy and rough with her siblings. She'd seek stimulation by running and crashing into them.

Oddly enough, despite her amazing athleticism and grace in gymnastics, she was often clumsily bumping into people or things. She could spin without getting dizzy for as much as ten minutes at a time, but was incredibly sensitive to other stimulation—the feeling of a waistband, belt, or other clothing on her midriff was unbearable to her and made her wriggle and squirm. She wasn't able to stand the feeling of sleeping in pajamas or a nightgown, even on cold nights. After a few months of working with Julie, she was able to wear all kinds of clothing, both during the day and at night. In fact, she was finally able to wear the skirts to her school uniform without slouching them down on her hips.

Crashing into things (such as the Climbing and Crashing intervention) and deep pressure (such as the Squashy Sandwich intervention) calmed her. Blowing activities, like the Blow the House Down intervention used for Ethan, Ice Cream from Chapter Three, and Balloon Blowing and Nok 'Em Down 'N' Roll 'Em from Chapter Two, also proved very helpful for Julie. Rubbing a nailbrush or even sandpaper on her skin also relaxed her and helped her develop her tactile sense. This helps by alerting the sensory receptors of the nervous system. In effect, it tells them, "Hey, wake up and smell the coffee."

Although these and other activities may arouse the system, some children respond differently. In such children, it may instead calm the sensory system by giving it the particular amount of satisfying stimulation the child's nervous system craves.

Within five months Julie was not only able to wear clothes without complaining, she was calmer, had far fewer tantrums, and was able to control her chatter. Her parents were no longer battling for control, and her siblings were no longer needed to compete with her for their parents' attention, at least not most of the time. And most importantly, Julie's mom felt confident and competent while parenting her, even when Julie's siblings were present, while previously she had felt unable to focus on Julie and her siblings at the same time.

•••

Rock 'N' Reach

This intervention gives children deep pressure in flexion-mode, as well as periods of extension. Children who are usually in extension actually need to go into flexion, but they aren't conscious of this at all. Rock 'N' Reach will help calm your child so that she doesn't need as much stimulation. This popular exercise is usually done on an exercise ball; however, I find that my lap version, with the hugging brings a warm connection to parent and child.

1. Sit on the floor and hold your child in your lap. Her bottom should be in your lap, with her legs, torso, and head curved into the flexion or gentle fetal position.

2. Wrap your arms around your child using deep, firm, but not overwhelming pressure. Rock back and forth, counting at least to ten, or singing the ABCs or another rhythmic counting song.

3. Stop and gently help your child into the extension position: legs out and torso, head, and arms back, hanging down.

4. Your child reaches for a puzzle piece behind her on the floor, just an inch or so beyond where she can naturally reach without stretching extensively.

5. When she curls back up onto your lap, she can place the puzzle piece on a table in front of you (to her side).

6. To upgrade the intervention and make it more challenging, try repeating on a low chair, and eventually a chair of typical height, so your child's arms and hands can hang even further down in extension. In this case you may choose to place the puzzle piece either on the floor or a short table. Dropping down a longer distance is scarier for some children, more thrilling for others. If you've got a child who is a risk-taker, start on a regular chair. Give them that intense thrill and rush they crave. (You'll need more abdominal strength.)

Optional: Try using a lower or higher chair, and a smaller or larger puzzle pieces. By adjusting the equipment, you make the activity easier or more challenging.

Special Equipment: Puzzle pieces.

Pointers: The puzzle piece gives your child a motivation to stretch out and really extend. To challenge your child, you may move the piece a bit further back occasionally, so she really has to reach. Placing the piece in the puzzle is its own reward. Or have her choose a card, as in the game of Go Fish. Use your imagination to come up with new ideas, and be sure to email them to me so we can share them with other parents on my blog at OTThrive.com.

Rock 'N' Reach is similar to Hat Trick in Chapter Two, and you can use either one, depending on your child's preference.

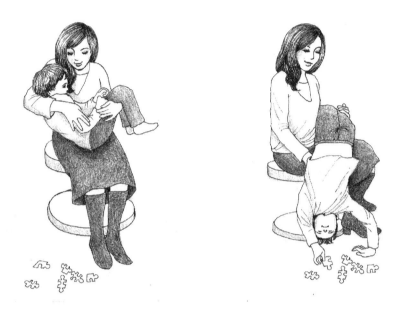

Rock 'N' Reach Steps 1 and 2   Rock 'N' Reach Steps 3 and 4

•••

Getting Out of Jail/Getting Into Jail

Getting Out of Jail gave Julie the input she craved. Once satisfied, Julie no longer sought as much sensory input and stopped pummeling her siblings. Your Heat-Seeking Missile may no longer squash babies by holding them too tightly or handle them too roughly, and may no longer push, bite, or hit.

1. Hold your child in your lap, as in Rock 'N' Reach, in a flexion position. Hold your arms tightly around her.

2. Tell her to try and get out of jail! She should use her shoulders and legs and torso to exert outward pressure in order to escape. Allow her to struggle and break through.

3. For Getting Into Jail, place two sofas, padded mats or chairs, facing each other. A pile of pillows behind each of you will work well, too.

4. Place an exercise-type ball or pillow between you and your child as you both kneel on the floor, facing each other.

5. Now, you and your child lean in and push with your torsos. You can use your arms to steady the ball if you are using one, but don't use them to push it. For a pillow, you won't need to use your arms. Each of you tries to put the other into jail by pushing against the ball with your torsos. Whoever hits the sofa or cushions behind them, loses!

Special Equipment: Exercise ball or pillow; carpeted floor or mats; sofas, chairs, or pillows to fall onto.

Pointers: Make it fun! For Getting Into Jail, tell your child you're putting her into jail because she was jaywalking or eating pizza while standing on her head. Go ahead and ask her why she's sending you to jail. Be sure to brush up on your jail jokes!

Here's one to get you started:

Judge: I'll have to give you three days in jail or one hundred dollars.

Prisoner: I'll take the hundred dollars, your honor.

Getting Into Jail Step 5
•••

Shift and Lift

This intervention helps your child sit in a chair without fidgeting. It can also help children who don't like to wear underwear or don't like the feeling of pants or skirts on their midriff. It uses a piece of equipment, which was introduced to me by Kim Barthel, called a Hokki stool. A Hokki stool is able to wobble without tipping over—perfect for children who need to move a lot in order to stay calm and focused.

Often called a "wiggle seat," a balance cushion, such as the one made by Isokinetics, is a less expensive alternative. I also offer a third variation of this exercise, which requires no equipment at all.

1. Your child sits on the Hokki stool or on the balance cushion.
2. She shifts from one haunch to the other in a rocking motion. Each time she "shifts and lifts" to the left, she hikes her left hip up and bends her left shoulder down, so in effect, she does a mild crunch on her left side. She does the same on the right side. The child switches back and forth, not too fast, just at a steady rhythm. This can be done more slowly or more quickly, it's up to your child, whatever she's comfortable doing. She should do this for five minutes daily.

3. In another version, your child sits with her knees bent and on the floor and her backside on her heels, on a soft rug or padded mat (see illustration).

Special Equipment: Hokki stool or balance cushion. A padded mat or rug if using the sitting version.

Pointers: Start with shifting and lifting for one minute, then increase incrementally until your child can do five minutes. Do this while your child's attention is otherwise engaged: read her a book, allow her to watch her favorite video, chew gum or listen to upbeat music she likes.

Shift and Lift Step 3

• • •

Personal Best

This is an easy intervention that you can personalize with your Heat-Seeking Missile. For Julie, we used cartwheels. For your child it could be somersaults, crab-walks, skipping rope, jumping jacks, or other high-energy physical activity that requires a bit of skill and endurance. The key is to choose an activity your child likes. Your child competes with herself and this enables her to experience motivation, achievement, and competition in a non-threatening manner. It also gives her the high-energy activity she craves.

1. Ask your child how many cartwheels or chosen activity she can do in at least one minute. Use a timer on a phone, watch, or egg timer to time her.

2. When she is done, ask her if she thinks she can beat her personal best and do a higher number of cartwheels (or chosen activity), in one minute.

Special Equipment: None, unless your child's chosen activity demands it (such as a jump rope or a trapeze).

Pointers: Your child may be able to do five or more minutes of her chosen activity; let her ability determine the duration of the Personal Best activity.

•••

Julie's mom is a bright, energetic woman, and like many parents I know, very hard on herself. Even while the situation at home was obviously improving, she'd still blame and shame herself, especially on the occasions where she "lost it." She'd tell herself that she was at fault, and was not a good mom.

Together we worked on the idea that improvement in any area of life is about the process of trying to do better, and that imperfections are expected, accepted, and okay. If we can stop being so judgmental of ourselves, we will also stop being judgmental of others—including our kids. It was also helpful for Julie's mom to sometimes take a time out. She'd tell the kids she was going to her room, or she'd take a drink of water and do breathing exercises—whatever she needed to feel more centered. When her four young children got too much for her to handle, I suggested she do her best to take some time for herself. She loved to sink into a hot bath or go for a brisk walk. If she wasn't able to carve out some time, she could carve out a bit of space. Even just putting herself in another room for a few minutes helped.

•••

When **Maddy** first came to see me, at age fifteen, she was in tenth grade. It was obvious she was bright, but she was functioning academically several years below grade level. With commitment to the use of a variety of therapies over time, and a lot of love, Maddy was able to move up to grade level. There were times Maddy did not want to do the interventions. There were times she asked me to intervene for her with her teachers; for example, she wanted me to ask them if she could skip a class a certain day. If I didn't agree that not doing an intervention or skipping a class would be beneficial for her, I'd tell her so. Sometimes I agreed with her, sometimes I didn't, but at the end of the day, through body language and verbal affirmations, I showed Maddy I still cared deeply about her and I wasn't going to abandon her. This is key!

Maddy wrote a poem that reminds me of the importance of the message in this beautiful quote about the power of love, from teacher and therapist, mentor and friend, Kimberly Barthel: "I may say yes, I may say no, but always I love you."

I received this poem from Maddy after we'd worked together for about a year. Maddy told me that Part II was written about eight months after Part I.

•••

Explaining
Part I

Something to say, that I'd like to express
Not quite clear, I'll try nonetheless.

It's hard to describe, too hard to explain
'Cuz it's all going on, inside MY brain.

It's all hidden, you cannot see
It takes place inside of me.

When I'm sitting on that school chair,
The one that greets me each morn with fear.

When I see it, I wanna throw a fit,
"Why can't I, in you just sit?"

The girl in the back, on the side and in the front,
They can sit there, like no great stunt.

But when I sit down, my legs hit the floor,
Now's the time, no moving—no more!

I can't not move, and just sit there,
I need to repeat it, like a reminder.

It may sound odd, but it's really true,
These little talks, really go through.

"Don't move, don't flick, don't tick—JUST SIT!
Be like everyone else, for a lil' bit!"

There's like this thing, it doesn't stop,
It makes me wanna skip, jump and hop.

It's like an itch, unitchable,
It's so itchy, it's horrible.

It keeps on tingling, an annoying tingle,
It is every minute, EVERY single.

Is it her too, or only me,
Sitting there so jittery?!?

I want to throw my hands up in despair,
I want to say, "I can't do this, it's not fair."

I want to fall apart and cry,
But I DON'T do that, I give it another try!

So, when is the time, when I do say
That it's not me, so it's okay!

I tried my best, I did all I should,
And now I know, not everyone COULD.

Part II

I feel so content
And now satisfied
A relaxed feeling
From deep inside

It's a feeling so real
One can't understand
Unless it was you
That was holding my hand

I was lucky enough
To have you as my OT
And become who I am now
The best I can be

Was it all that blowing?!?
Or the non-stop spinning?!?
Maybe your words
Or your face that's always grinning!

In every exercise
Stretch and routine
Always the positive
Somehow was seen

Best of all
You showed you cared
And so my feelings
Were openly shared

Discovering my needs
Together we did find
Understanding it all
And clearing my mind

What I can and can't do
You helped me to know
And that challenges in life
Were a time to grow

You gave me so much
You gave me it all
You allowed me to stand
On my own feet so tall!

You gave me the gift
That no one else can give
The proper tools
And the clarity in how I live.

Chapter Five: The Squeaky Wheel

Talky!

The Squeaky Wheel copes with anxiety and other uncomfortable feelings and sensations by the act of constantly sharing thoughts, ideas, feelings, memories, worries, and so on. Sometimes he talks because it distracts him from the turmoil he feels as a resulting of the difficulty he has making sense of the world. Sometimes he talks because his inner world isn't making sense. Sometimes he talks to alleviate feelings of disconnection from others. Other words and phrases you could also use to describe your Squeaky Wheel might include some of these:

- Gabby
- Chatty
- Loquacious
- Annoying
- Buzzing
- Motormouth
- Yakking

- Rambling
- Squeaky
- Geyser
- Verbose
- Babbling
- Chatterbox

And of course, *Talky*.

• • •

The Squeaky Wheel usually overlaps with other behavioral issues, especially, but not limited to the Heat-Seeking Missile and The Princess and the Pea. Your chatterbox finds it very hard to be silent. But a lot is going on besides the apparent need to chat. There may be functional and/or emotional reasons a child talks incessantly. There are often both.

A child may chatter away because he is "in his head" and doesn't have a sense of being in his body—he feels disconnected from the neck down.

This may be compounded by anxiety, hyperactivity, or a dysregulated sensory system. If a child is having a hard time making sense of what he's feeling and experiencing, this can be quite anxiety-producing.

Tyler from Chapter Three was in a state of constant alert and mirrored his mother's anxiety. His chatting was both functional (caused by his dysregulated system) and emotional (caused by his need for constant approval from his mom and other adults). Talking helped him release tension. It was also his way of trying to feel more connected to others. Also, when Tyler talked, he experienced a greater sense of self.

Julie, in Chapter Four, was also a Squeaky Wheel, though for her the primary cause was functional with only some minor emotional components. Her dysregulated system needed constant stimulation and talking constantly was one way of self-stimulating. This is because using the mouth can help regulate the nervous system—talking, eating, sucking, chewing, and biting nails, pencils, and other objects, may help a child feel less tense by giving him the level of stimulation he needs. Also, the mouth is used to stabilize vision. When the eyes need to work harder, the nearby mouth muscles may be drafted to help stabilize weak vision muscles.

A chatty child may also exhibit an overabundance of other oral behaviors. Using the mouth may be soothing for adults, too. Adults may eat, drink, or smoke, to calm themselves.

•••

Stephanie, a smiling eight-year-old with olive skin and large brown eyes, was a chatty child. She came to see me accompanied by her mother, Helen, a psychiatric nurse. Helen had a high-pressure job, and her pregnancy with Stephanie was not an easy one (she was born prematurely). Helen had recognized early on that Stephanie needed some help and she had been taking her to another occupational therapist for almost five years. Helen saw some improvements, but Stephanie, at eight, was still orally fixated—constantly biting, chewing, and sucking her clothing, pencils, toys and so on. She even ate crayons and books. She was a sloppy eater in general, and had a hard time concentrating in the classroom.

The oral fixation was Helen's primary concern. She described Stephanie as a delightful child who needed a lot of attention and had the occasional fear of the unknown. Stephanie was, indeed, a delight. She was very playful and talked quite a bit, in a friendly way, but I could see her brain was working overtime and it was obvious that her chatter was driven by anxiety, and maybe even fear. Everything had to be PERFECT, otherwise Stephanie's anxiety would ratchet up. Her mom confirmed that this plentiful chatter was because of anxiety, but that Stephanie was way less anxious at the Thrive OT Sensory Gym than she usually was in new places. In fact, once she spent some time in our large Lycra swing, she began to calm down and was able to stop talking.

I explained to Stephanie's mom that her daughter's excessive talkativeness was actually part of her oral fixation. I also described what I found from my evaluation: that Stephanie's behavioral issues had both functional and emotional components. Though at first, Helen was a bit reluctant to address the chatter as well as the other oral behaviors, she finally agreed when I demonstrated that talking was directly related to biting and chewing. What do these behaviors have in common? The mouth!

Also, I wanted to find out if Stephanie's biting, chewing, and sucking was simply an oral fixation, or if she was biting as a way to stabilize her eye movement. I explained to Helen that the mouth may be considered the center of the body. It can help stabilize the body; for example, people often grit their teeth or clench their jaws when they are doing tasks with their hands, legs, or body. In addition, the mouth specifically helps stabilize the eyes.

You can try this yourself: Clench your teeth and you'll notice that it centers and stabilizes your vision. Keeping your mouth slightly open and your jaw relaxed, roll your eyeballs in circles. Now, clench your teeth and try rolling in the same circles. Your eye circles will most likely be tighter and more controlled with a clenched jaw.

A brief period of close observation and assessment confirmed part of the reason why Stephanie bit her pencils, even her books, during class: she was trying to stabilize her eyes with her mouth. Lack of focused vision was one of the reasons she was having such a difficult time focusing in school. Now that I had determined that Stephanie's oral symptoms had both emotional (anxiety, worry, fear) and functional (visual challenges) causes, we could create a personalized treatment plan for her. The plan would include a series of achievable goals, and interventions that would help her meet these goals.

Part of my plan for Stephanie included doing some inner-core strengthening to help her develop better breathing habits, which would also help her relax and focus. Any of the inner-core and blowing interventions in the previous chapters also may be helpful for a Squeaky Wheel.

In Stephanie's case, once we implemented a plan that included a variety of interventions both at the Thrive OT sensory gym and at home with her mom, there was rapid improvement. She began to be able to calm herself down, she began staying focused in class (without a constant need to fidget), for longer and longer amounts of time, and although she still occasionally bit her pencil, she had stopped eating objects like crayons and books.

Most of all, her incessant talking had slowed down. Yes, she still was a talkative child, but her chatter wasn't as constant, nor as grating or shrill. She wasn't as dependent on her mother to supply enormous amounts of attention and was able to have age-appropriate conversations with other children for the first time.

•••

Yummies

In their helpful book, *Out of the Mouths of Babes: Discovering the Developmental Significance of the Mouth* (Pileated Press), Sheila Frick, Ron Frick, Patricia Oetter, and Eileen W. Richter offer several suggestions for activities which can help with oral fixation, biting, chewing, and chatter. In this group of interventions I call "Yummies," numbers two, three, and five (below) are inspired by ideas found in *Out of the Mouths of Babes*.

1. Swipe the sides of your child's tongue with lemon or mint extract once or twice a day. You may dilute the extract if it causes stomachache. Place a drop or two on a cotton swab or your finger, and swipe.

2. Especially during snack time, give your child crunchy objects to bite and chew, such as hard, thick pretzels; hard crackers or melba toast; or mini ice cubes.

3. Give your child sour tasting foods and drinks: pickles, straight cranberry juice (unsweetened concentrate diluted with water), and grapefruit juice. Let her drink from straws, especially narrow ones, and bottles with sports caps. The Citra Citrus Sipper from Chapter Four is a good choice, too.

4. Give your child one to two pieces of frozen gum to chew, or frozen squeezable yogurt tubes.

5. Give your child thick liquids to sip with a straw, such as smoothies.

Special Equipment: Straws, sports bottles; mini ice cube makers, available from Bed, Bath, and Beyond and other stores; Citra Citrus Sipper™.

Pointers: Mix it up! If your child has a favorite, stick with it for a while, but try new Yummies occasionally. Offer these as a preventative measure—before or during transitions, stressful events, or at other times. If you need to, you can also offer these while she's already talking nonstop or biting/chewing/sucking.

•••

Calm Press

Calm Press, a wonderful idea from Kim Barthel, and also very similar to Chinese acupressure techniques, utilizes basic pressure to help calm and relax. It's easy to do, and older children and adolescents may even be able to do it themselves.

1. Visualize each eye as a clock. Using the pad of your thumb, press gently at the twelve o'clock position above each eyebrow. Hold for the count of eight.

2. Then, apply a bit of pressure outside the eye, at the three o'clock (left eye) and nine o'clock (right eye) positions. Hold for the count of eight at the temple area.

3. Finally, do the same with the top of the cheek bone beneath each eye at the six o'clock position. Be sure to press on the bone, not in the socket). Make sure you press right in the center of the cheek bone—you may use the pupil to "line up" the spot. Hold for the count of eight.

Special Equipment: None.

Pointers: You may repeat as often as needed. You may also want to teach your child to do Calm Press herself.

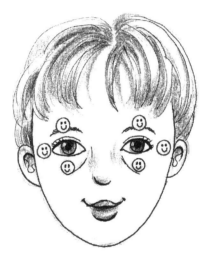

Calm Press

•••

Critter Quest

Critter Quest is based on an eye exercise by Hans G. Furth and Harry Wachs, from their wonderful book, *Thinking Goes to School* (Oxford University Press, 1975). It helps with eye movement (tracking). You can do it with your child, or two children can do it taking turns.

1. You're the (imaginary) critter. Using a low, relaxed voice (it can be a funny voice to attract your child's attention and enhance the game aspect of this intervention), narrate and describe your imaginary position as you inch your way slowly around the molding, wainscoting, or baseboard of a room. You might say things like, "Now I'm moving forward to that *dusty* corner, now I'm turning right and climbing slowly up the door frame." You may move forward, reverse, stop, climb, descend, etc.
2. Your child is the "tracker." Her job is to follow the critter with her eyes.
3. Variation: Use a flashlight or laser pointer along with your imaginative narration.

Special Equipment: Your imagination! You can also use a flashlight or laser pointer if you are trying the variation.

Pointers: Make sure your critter moves at a comfortable speed. Too slow or too fast may be frustrating for your child.

• • •

Yo-Yo Button

Yo-Yo Button is based on another exercise from *Thinking Goes to School*. It helps your child's eyes work together as a team, enabling them to function better in a classroom. For example, your child will find it easier to switch from board to teacher to her desktop, and still stay focused. In Stephanie's case, sometimes mouth movements and oral fixation were used as an attempt to stabilize her eyes. For example, sometimes a child will chew on a pencil in order to help her focus her vision.

1. Unwind the string from a yo-yo. Thread a large button onto the string, and tie knot to secure, as in the illustration. The button should be a solid color which contrasts with the color of the yo-yo.

2. Your child stands perpendicular to you. Spread out your arms so that the yo-yo string is about two to three feet long, and the button is at the end. Hold the button end two inches from your child's face at eye level.

3. Ask your child to switch her vision back and forth when she hears your directions: yo-yo, button, yo-yo, button, and so forth.

Special Equipment: A yo-yo and a button.

Pointers: Hold the button approximately two inches in front of the bridge of your child's nose. You may experiment by going more slowly or more quickly, and changing how far the yo-yo is from the eye. Use a pretty or cool-looking button, and/or change the button every so often to add motivation. You can also try using a different object. I once tied a party blower onto the string instead of a button, and the kids loved it.

Yo-Yo Button
•••

Stephanie's mom, Helen, asked me what to do when Stephanie displayed fear or anxiety. I suggested that she not necessarily attempt to fix the situation, but rather she should sit with her daughter's distress, validate it, and show empathy with intense affect (while remaining calm inside). Not every problem needs to be fixed.

Over time, things became less scary for Stephanie as she developed the ability to regulate herself. By verbalizing what Stephanie was experiencing, and allowing them both to just "sit with their feelings," Helen imparted to Stephanie the skills she needed to deal with discomfort. And therefore, when uncomfortable feelings did surface, it was no longer a crisis. Stephanie began to believe she could get through situations that might be uncomfortable or unpleasant.

• • •

Brian, the oldest of four, was about to turn six, yet he was still sucking his thumb and mouthing collars and sleeves of his shirts and jackets, as well as books, toys, and almost anything in his path. He had poor oral muscle tone and found chewing difficult, but loved to eat soft sweet treats (he could eat them all day if allowed). Brian also seemed to miss a lot of social cues, although he was very intelligent and also managed to be patient with his siblings, who adored him.

Brian's parents had several concerns. His neediness was a big issue for his mom, Alicia. He was desperate for Alicia's attention, and in order to get it, he talked. Brian sought his mom's acknowledgment—about anything and everything. During the first few months we worked together, he constantly checked in with Alicia, saying, "Mom, look at this! Mom, look at that! Mom, look at me!"

Even if Alicia's attention was elsewhere, he'd still be focused on her. He'd say to me, "I gotta show Mommy." He was preoccupied with getting his emotional needs met by Alicia even in absentia. Brian never really felt his mom approved of him. Though she'd put on a happy face for her son, Alicia would often turn away and look exasperated. It was frustrating to her that Brian wasn't like everyone else, and it showed. Brian was sensitive to this, so even when his mom was focused on him, it was never enough. Alicia also missed some cues as to what Brian needed, so part of what she and I decided to focus on was how to be more positively present for him.

Talking wasn't the only way Brian tried to regulate his system; he also sucked his thumb and "zoned out." The intensity of his needs could overwhelm him, so shutting down his thoughts helped him get some rest from anxiety and tension. As long as he was sucking on his thumb or chewing something (and sometimes rocking), he could sit calmly or play quietly. In other words, he was using his oral fixation to regulate his nervous system and calm his thoughts. If I could help Brian's brain think less intensely and help him understand and connect with his feelings, he'd feel less desperate and have less need to talk, bite, chew, and suck his thumb.

After evaluating Brian, I created a plan to address his parents' many concerns, with an emphasis on his oral fixation and talkativeness. Alicia also agreed it would be helpful if she could learn to better pick up on Brian's cues for connection and interaction when he was in a quieter space, before he launched into chatter, despite the fact that it would be a challenge for her because she was so busy with her other children.

Part of our treatment plan included Therapeutic Listening™, which we began right away. In Therapeutic Listening, we use specially created music to help with a variety of sensory processing disorders. In Brian's case, after I chose the appropriate music, I'd place specialized headphones designed for Therapeutic Listening, on Brian while he was swinging in the Lycra swing. Swinging and rocking motions were very calming for Brian. Over time, this and other interventions began to help him to think more calmly and tune in to his sensory systems. His aimless chatter and constant reaching out for mom became less and less frequent.

At home, I asked his mother to play Therapeutic Listening CDs for him with good-quality headphones. At other times, she used a metronome with seventy or ninety beats per minute to help Brian focus. I also recommended Brian's parents buy a Hokki stool for home use and recommended that they ask the teacher if he could sit on one at school. Within a month, Brian showed improvement, and after three months, it was clear that his mind was quieter and his body, more relaxed. He began to pick up on social cues and interact more with friends. He began to be able to chew his food better, and didn't demand to eat sweet puddings and cakes as often. He still did occasionally suck his thumb, but it was far less frequently.

Most gratifying for Alicia was that Brian no longer demanded her attention constantly. He began to speak more thoughtfully and express his feelings. The improvement was dramatic, noticed by his tutor, teachers, and, of course, parents. And though his peers may not have articulated it, they obviously felt that Brian was better able to connect with them, so he had more play dates and a budding new social life.

● ● ●

Flashlight Fun

Flashlight Fun is made up of two interventions based on exercises in *Thinking Goes to School*. They both help to strengthen ocular movement, which is related to the mouth.

1. Flashlight Fun Tag requires two flashlights with different colored lights (such as one red, one blue). You can play with your child or have another child near the same age play with him. In a darkened room, you both shine your lights on the wall, and someone is chosen to be "it." Whoever is "it" tries to evade the capture of his light. Once he's caught, the other person becomes "it," and he tries to catch the other person's light. You can play with two or three players.

2. Flashlight Fun Leapfrog: In this intervention, you call out objects, and your child shines his flashlight (any color) on the object as quickly as possible. You can increase the speed as his skill improves.

Special Equipment: Flashlights. You may use one or two layers of colored cellophane placed over the flashlights in Flashlight Fun Tag, or you may purchase colored flashlights.

Pointers: In both Tag and Leapfrog, you may play with as many players as you have flashlights, if your child finds it fun to do so (and doesn't find increased participation anxiety-provoking).Your child can stand on an uneven or wobbly surface such as a couch, to make it more challenging.

•••

Heavy and Soft

This is an incredibly calming intervention with several easy variations.

1. Your child lies down in bed, on the floor (exercise mat or carpet), or on a firm sofa.
2. Place a weighted pillow, or a regular bed pillow with a heavy book, such as a dictionary, on top. Cover with a favorite blanket if your child prefers.
3. Variation: Child sits leaning against a wall. He holds a weighted ball. A favorite blanket covering him creates a safe, cocoon-like space.

Special Equipment: Weighted pillow or pillows; weighted ball; blanket other weighted objects. You can play relaxing music or CDs of nature sounds, such as waterfalls, waves, or rainstorms.

Pointers: This can be done at bedtime, to help a child transition to sleep. Or, it can be done when your child is anxious or overly talkative. You may choose to use a few objects on several areas of the body.

•••

Roly-Poly

This activity gives your child deep pressure which helps him become more aware of his body.

1. On a very large piece of spandex, a flexible area rug, or a blanket, your child begins to roll around and around, while you help him roll up inside the material.
2. His head should stick out so he can breathe.

Special Equipment: Rug, spandex, or blanket.

Pointers: The material should be large enough that when rolled, it doubles your child's width. The heavy, all-over cocooning or swaddling effect is very relaxing. Some kids like their arms out, some prefer them to be tucked in.

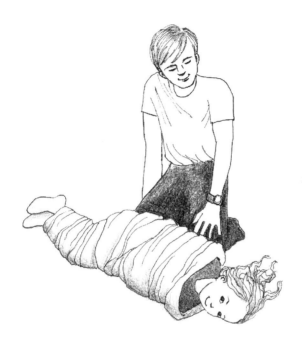

Roly Poly
•••

Spa Glove

This intervention uses spa gloves, those inexpensive, soft loofah-like bath gloves available in every drugstore. When used during massage, they help your child get a sense of where he is in space and tune into his body—not just his brain. This intervention helps calm your child down, which means less talking!

1. Using spa gloves, on bare skin, rub his body, arms, legs, back, and face, chin, mouth, and belly if he is comfortable with this.
2. After the massage, pull gently on each limb. (See Hand Hugs and Stretch in Chapter Three.)
3. Variation: Try sandpaper, a body brush or soft hairbrush, or other textured materials for the massage. Your child might have different preferences depending on how he is feeling. Not every child will enjoy every texture; some may find specific ones to be very irritating.

Special Equipment: Spa gloves (the softer, synthetic type; real loofah might be too rough). You can buy the gloves online at drugstore.com. Or you can use paintbrushes or sponges.

Pointers: Brush in the direction of the body hair, not against it. Use deep pressure, and gently pull the limb at the same time.

•••

The other activities from this chapter were also helpful to Brian. Alicia, Brian's mom, was disappointed that Brian wasn't a typical kid and unlike others his age. Brian was sensitive to the fact that although his mother's words sounded positive, her disappointment showed in her facial expressions. I suggested she start journaling between sessions in order to get her feelings of disappointment out on paper. This lessened the occurrence of her negative facial expressions. It was also helpful for her to find activities/ interests to do with Brian that she and he both enjoyed. This way it was easier to show him how she genuinely enjoyed spending time with him.

Chapter Six: Taking Care of You

You know those oxygen masks that the flight attendants demonstrate how to use on every flight you take? You are instructed to first put the mask on yourself before putting it on your child. The reason is simple: if you aren't able to breathe and function well, you won't be able to help your child. Sometimes, in our desire to help our child, we forget that we must take care of our own emotional and physical needs first. A happy, healthy parent feels ready to take on parenting challenges. Conversely, the more we neglect our own needs, the more difficult parenting becomes. Whether or not you follow through, you *know* that it's good to take care of your physical needs by eating right, resting, exercising, and so on. But it's just as important to take care of your emotional and spiritual needs.

I've worked with hundreds of parents just like you who've struggled with their child's behavior, as well as other life challenges. Some find it hard to accept their child's personality. I've met many mothers and fathers who feel frustrated or disappointed with their child, and many who are even ashamed of them. More than a few are angry—at their child, at themselves, at the situation.

Parents have told me that they feel really stuck. Some have told me they secretly feel that they hate their child. I've had parents tell me they felt sad or anxious much of the time; they felt stuck in an emotional rut and felt guilty because this affected their ability to interact with their child. And, they felt bad about themselves.

Parenting a child with behavioral challenges can be draining, but it doesn't have to be. No matter how you feel, believe you are capable of having a more enjoyable relationship with your child. I've worked with parents who felt they'd never be happy about their child, yet, a few months down the road, they experienced delight and pleasure from the parent-child relationship. When your needs are met, when you develop self-knowledge, your relationship with your child is strengthened.

•••

Mindfulness

Before reading the next sentence, take a deep breath and allow yourself to exhale slowly. You may notice you feel more relaxed. Paying attention to the breath helps you feel calm in nearly any situation. One simple, calming breath technique is to inhale for the count of six, hold the breath for four, and exhale for the count of eight or ten. Once you feel more relaxed, touch base with yourself.

Ask yourself and make notes here:

What do I hear?

What do I see?

What do I smell?

What am I touching/What do I feel?

Can I feel my heartbeat?

What is going on around me?

As you notice each answer, you will slowly begin to experience what is called "mindfulness." A simple definition of mindfulness is to *live with/feel an awareness of the present moment.* Being present in the moment helps you as you interact with others in your life, including your child. When you are mindful, you really see and hear your child with a new level of awareness. Your understanding of your relationship will deepen.

•••

Know Thyself

In order to deeply understand what your child needs, to really "get" where your child is coming from, and how he experiences the world around him, it's essential that you know who you are: what makes you tick, what brings you down, what uplifts you, what turns you off. When we know who we are, we are more open to seeing beyond the surface in others. But in order to understand who we are, we have to take the time to do so. By learning more about who you are and how you feel about yourself, your child, and life in general, you'll be able to interact more effectively—and lovingly—with your child.

• • •

A Forgotten Child in a Parent's Body

There's a well-known saying: If it's hysterical, it's historical. In other words, if something really pushes your buttons, it's because the situation is probably bringing up issues from your past. For example, if, as you watch your child struggle to make friends and fail, or stumble clumsily in dance class, you feel anger or shame, it's possible that you were judged as a child. Perhaps you were taught that being popular or graceful was extremely important and without these things, you had little worth. Maybe you felt unappreciated no matter how hard you tried to meet a parent's or teacher's expectations. Nothing—nothing!—brings up issues from our childhood like becoming a parent.

When you feel these turbulent emotions, you really can benefit from giving yourself your own time-out, in the form of a mindfulness-break. Take a few deep breaths, or use the six/four/eight breath, above. Make a call to a friend, pray, and do whatever you need to, to try and return to your calm, deep center.

• • •

How Do I Really Feel?

The emotions we experience and the feelings we have about our child and ourselves can run the gamut from wonderful, uplifting, comforting, or calm, to anxiety-producing, unpleasant, or even unbearable. You might ask yourself, "Why am I not able to feel good about my child and my relationship with him (at least, most of the time)?" The good news is: Feelings can and do change. Though you may feel it's true, you are not stuck with negative feelings forever. *While feelings live in the heart, they're shaped by the mind.* By using your mind to become more aware of your feelings, you gain understanding. For example, think about and reflect on what's really pushing your buttons—whether it's your child's tantrum, his shrill voice, or other behavior. Does his behavior feel like a criticism or rejection of your ability to parent, or a rejection of you?

•••

Compassion, Not Judgment

It is fairly common for parents to feel that the way their child acts is a reflection on them. And in part, it's true. But children are more than miniature proofs of our parenting skills, family culture, genes, and abilities. They are their own unique, individual selves. I, myself struggle with this, especially as an occupational therapist who specializes in children's behavioral issues. I imagine if my kids are not well behaved, how will that look to others? Will they judge me negatively as a parent or a therapist? (And, will I judge myself negatively?) I remind myself that my goal is to do the best I can with the tools I have. I remind myself to resist internal and external pressures to be a perfect parent.

If I can accept myself and my imperfections, then I will accept the imperfections of my children (and other people). If I resist the fact that I have imperfections, if I shame and blame myself, then I will also be unable to accept my children's imperfections, and shame and blame them. If I look at the good things about myself, I'll focus on the good things in my children.

Author and speaker Brené Brown says, "You can't shame or belittle people into changing their behaviors." This even applies to you! If you have feelings of anxiety, anger, annoyance, hopelessness, and other negative feelings around your child's behavior, recognizing that you have those feelings is a tremendous first step toward healing those feelings. But shaming or belittling yourself because you have those feelings won't work.

Give yourself permission to be perfectly okay with being imperfect. The less you shame and belittle yourself, the less you "beat yourself up," the more you'll be accepting of your child's or another person's shortcomings. One of the miracles that occurs when you take the time to understand yourself is simply this: *by becoming aware of why you feel the way you do, your interactions with your child automatically become more satisfying*—even if you are *not* actively trying to change things.

For example, if you find yourself overwhelmed, ashamed, or even panicky because of your child's tantrums, you might discover that the deep reason this bothers you is because it makes you feel like a failure as a parent. Perhaps these feelings of failure might be rooted in shame because someone you respect, love, or are in a relationship with has told you that if your kids misbehave, it means you're not a good parent. When you become aware of the source of your feelings, you will find yourself gradually able to become calmer when your child has tantrums. But if you feel ashamed of your child's behavior, then you will feel the need to control him, either by physical or emotional means. The desire for control comes from the need for perfection, and the need for perfection is rooted in fear and shame.

However, when you understand that your reaction is in many ways about you, what you believe and feel (and often rooted in your personal history or social norms), you let go of shaming and blaming. Of course, this is a simplified version of what occurs, but experience shows that self-discovery leads to better relationships. Understanding yourself might change the dance interaction with your child by only two degrees, but those two degrees will have huge ramifications over time. The slightest positive change is progress, and has a cumulative effect.

•••

Hearing Your Body's Song

If it's hard for you to identify your emotions and feelings, try paying attention to the physical signals your body is telling you. Our bodies let us know what we're really feeling, if we only slow down and listen to them. Below are some common expressions of intense emotion that occur. Note that body signals appear in more than one emotional category. In real life, we may experience more than one feeling at a time, too.

Annoyance and/or Disgust: Eye rolling, explosive or frequent sighs, groans, clenching of teeth or jaw, shudders, nausea, shaking of head, tense or shrill voice, curling of lip, desire to avoid touch of another person.

Anger: Clenching of teeth or jaw, difficulty swallowing, slight to extreme clenching of fists, rapid heartbeat, flaring nostrils, headache, dizziness, feelings of unreality or being separated from your "self" or "body," chest pain, feeling like your are going to explode, burning or freezing sensations in your body or head, sweating, red face.

Stress and Anxiety: Overwhelming tension, irritability, close to tears, rapid heartbeat, feeling frozen or stuck, lack of appetite or extreme munchies/hunger, indigestion, nail biting, constant physical ailments, obsessive thoughts/worries, insomnia, feelings of dread, feeling like your mind's gone blank/inability to think.

If you recognize any of these signs in yourself, don't be surprised. Everybody has feelings like these sometimes. It's when these feelings interfere with our ability to live joyful, fulfilling lives, or have a depleting effect on our relationships, that we want to make a greater effort to understand where they're coming from. When we're engaged in this process, it's important also to treat ourselves with compassion.

•••

The Best Laid Plans...

Sometimes I personally use step-by-step plans to parent my own children. I believe it's okay to have a plan, such as the kind taught in parenting courses. But, before I recommend a specific action plan for others, I prefer to get to know the parents and child. I need to see how the child processes sensory information, see where they're up to developmentally, and learn about their cognitive abilities. Also, I need to see how the parents and their child interact. So much depends on your family culture, your goals, and your child's particular challenges. I try to understand the child's underlying issues (such as his low frustration threshold, difficulty handling transitions, maintaining focus, irritability, black-and-white thinking, misinterpreting social cues, low self-esteem, seeking attention in inappropriate ways, or incapacity to understand another's point of view). A one-size-fits-all plan will not work in most cases.

When I do parent-coaching, I always explore, listen, and learn. Then together, parents and I are able to develop a plan that meets their and their child's needs. Our plan may include some traditional parenting-class tips and tricks, as well as creative, original responses to their unique situation.

•••

Time and Process

A lot of the parents who come to see me (but not all, by any means), are teachers, psychologists, social workers, psychiatrists, therapists, and others in health care. They have excellent techniques and have the know-how to teach and reach children. But their techniques aren't necessarily effective with their own child because their child's system isn't primed and ready to accept their intervention.

If you fall into this category, don't give up on all the valuable skills you've learned. You may have tried a specific technique a year ago with your child, and he may not have been ready for it. It may be time to re-evaluate your child's readiness and try again. Once your child's nervous system becomes more regulated, through the implementation of a personalized treatment plan including occupational therapy, you may find all those marvelous techniques, which work with other children, work with your child, too.

Remember that the healing process is your personalized opportunity for insight, growth, and connection. Just as the ultimate goal of life isn't perfection but the process, the goal of parenting is the process. It's not about becoming the perfect parent. The process includes the struggles and the successes—these both are necessary to enrich our character and understanding.

Developing patience is one of the greatest gifts you can give to yourself as a parent. It's also one of the greatest gifts you can give to your child. It is heartbreaking to see a child in therapy begin to make progress, but not meet the parents' personal timetable for progress. What some feel should take days or weeks might need months, or even years.

Remember: *There are often solutions, but your child has to be ready for them.*

For children with the behavioral challenges such as the ones listed in this book (and others), readiness happens at various stages. It's also helpful to keep in mind that interventions that provide benefits during one stage of the healing process may not work at another stage. That's because as your child grows and changes, his needs and abilities to integrate new information also changes. Although children might seem to develop in bursts and spurts, a lot of what appears to be sudden change may be months or more in the making. Generally, a child will have to work through one phase of growth and healing in order to be ready for the next.

•••

Be a Well-Digger, Not a Firefighter

You've developed patience and have come to more self-awareness. You've seen your relationship with your child unfold in a more positive way, and you know yourself and him better. Now it's time to dig deeper. Some parents are like firefighters, regularly putting out behavioral fires. In some situations, finding a hydrant, grabbing a hose, and squelching that blaze may be absolutely necessary. But what if you could connect to the actual water supply on a permanent basis? How would you go about doing it? Why, dig, of course!

For example, if your child likes to have a cup of water at bedtime and he insists you bring him a different cup, do some digging. Sometimes it might be easier (and even a good choice) to put out the fire by simply going down and getting him the cup he prefers or just saying no to a change of cup. Either of these responses might be an appropriate course of action. Sometimes parents are so tired at the end of a long day, they might put an end to the bedtime complaints by shouting (or punishing).

But there's another alternative: dig a well. At a neutral time (not at bed time), you might want to articulate suggestions that can help your child become aware of the underlying reasons he feels dissatisfied, which can help him grow and change. Why does he want a different cup instead of the green one you've given him? Is it because he's trying to stay awake a bit longer? Or is it something else? Perhaps he thought he would have his old blue cup, and he feels uncomfortable when the reality is different from what he expected. Perhaps it's because the rim of the green cup isn't as smooth as his blue cup, and he finds the sensation unbearable.

An eight-year-old girl might come home from her second week in a new school and casually mutter, "I don't know if I have any friends." A firefighter will make a play date for her, purchase a trendy backpack, and stuff it with popular snacks—enough to share with everyone in her carpool. And there's nothing wrong with giving a child a material solution to solve problems; in fact, it may sometimes be necessary.

But when your daughter comes home with her lower lip trembling, a well-digger might suggest, with visible empathy, "It must hurt to feel like you don't have friends." Allowing the child to say, yes, she's hurting, without shaming or blaming her, is incredibly freeing for her (and for you, too). Without piling on blame or offering too many active solutions, this little girl will be far more likely able to develop compassion for herself, as well as empathy for others, including, down the road, her own children. Also, by having a conversation that involves listening to, instead of just talking to your child, you set the stage for your relationship with her to be more in sync.

• • •

In Sync

My mentor, Kimberly Barthell, teaches simple ways to get in sync with your child. She calls them "attunement parameters." Attunement parameters are easy communication techniques you can use to connect with your child.

Facial Expression

Facial Expression and Gesture: Show your child you really are interested in him, and validate his experience by your non-verbal affect, both with facial expressions and gestures. Look into his eyes in a friendly way, and moving your head slightly toward him when you and he speak; leaning your body toward him; stepping toward him; raising your shoulders; and so on.

Use your hands to emphasize or express connection. Give him a variety of non-verbal cues that show you are listening to him—and enjoying it! Did you know a forehead, eyebrows, and even a chin can convey interest, surprise, happiness, or excitement? (They also can show anger, frustration, and disappointment.)

If your child smiles, smile. If he frowns, frown slightly. Although you are matching his intensity with your visible affect, inside, you want to remain calm. Then your child will feel validated, yet he also will begin to mirror your inner calm. This nearly always happens. Also, when you mirror your child's feelings by using facial affect and gesture, you are validating him at a deeper level than if you just validate him verbally. He will feel that you care more deeply. Some children do not like direct eye contact; find other ways to make them feel that you are attuned to them (body contact, pitch of voice, and hand gestures are examples of this).

Verbal Expression: Validate your child verbally by using a sincere tone of voice; don't make light of what he says or what you say. Caring and interest can easily be expressed in your voice. Children have a hard time picking up some verbal cues, such as sarcasm or certain types of humor. If your child is a talkative Squeaky-Wheel type, try tucking your chin down and speaking in a deep and rhythmic, steady voice. Often your child will mirror you and respond with a lower-pitched, steadier voice of his own. This could take ten minutes, but it usually does happen.

However, if your child is really excited about something, your voice may mirror that excitement, too. The goal in this, and all the attunement parameters, is to express to your child that you are there with him, so he feels secure. In this way you can maintain an open, honest relationship.

After Ethan, a Heat-Seeking Missile, had been seeing me for a few months, his nervous system was primed. I knew it was time to give his mom the tools to parent him more effectively. We explored how she interacted with him when he expressed emotion. She had been able to mirror Ethan's positive, upbeat emotions, when he was happy or excited about something. But, when he was feeling anxious, negative, or over-reactive, she had been unable to mirror him effectively. His overreaction would cause her to shut down. Once Ethan's mom learned how to mirror her son's negative emotions while remaining calm, herself, he was able to calm down rather quickly.

Body Position and Body Contact: Allow your body to be open to the child: face him with arms uncrossed. Some children respond well to sitting shoulder to shoulder while touching arms and thighs. For some (like Hannah and her mom in Chapter Two), the best position is having the child sitting on your lap, not facing you. Sensitive children may react strongly to certain facial expressions. Hannah was quite sensitive and became anxious herself when her mother's face displayed signs of anxiety, such as a scrunched-up forehead. Hannah's mom gave her what she needed with body contact, rather than face-to-face interaction.

Affection: Showing affection probably seems obvious to you, but it's not to every parent. Some parents are so busy educating their child, that even though they deeply love their child, they forget to show simple love and warmth. They'd be surprised to hear that their child doesn't sense he's loved. Being warm, showing delight when your child comes home from school, touching his face and squeezing his hand, smiling, telling him that you love him with sincerity, placing a warm hand on his shoulder—all of these can change the parent-child relationship. There are debates about how many hugs a day are necessary for a child (adults need them, too), but many experts agree that eight hugs a day is one way to give a body what it needs.

Play: Playing with your child is also so important, sometimes even more important than helping him with his homework. Play is most beneficial when it's something you both enjoy doing. It might be taking a walk, coloring, or any age-appropriate activity you both like. You may enjoy playing music in the house and dancing. Tell your child that you can't wait to play that new game with him and that you're excited about spending time with him. Doing activities together that require you to take turns (such as board games or ball games) establishes a sense of give-and-take.

Doing fun activities where you have to use teamwork, such as being on the same team for charades or a treasure hunt, teaches your child sharing and helps you both take turns being in charge. Remember, you run the house, but when you are trying to get in sync with the child, giving up control during play helps you both bond. Besides, giving up some control can be a relief. The goal isn't to finish the game, but to enjoy the process of connecting to your child.

You tell your child with your actions and behavior that

I HEAR you.

I SEE you.

I FEEL you.

I WANT you.

I LOVE you.

I want to CONNECT with you, and I love it when you CONNECT with me.

•••

Resource Guide

Bibilography

Ayres, Anna J. Sensory Integration and Learning Disorders. Torrance, CA: Western Psychological Services, 1973.

Ayres, Anna J. Sensory Integration and the Child: Twenty-fifth Anniversary Edition. Torrance, CA: Western Psychological Services, 2005.

Barthel, Kimberly. Evidence and Art Merging Forces in Pediatric Therapy. Victoria, British Columbia: Labyrinth Journeys, 2004.

Blomberg, Harald and Moira Dempsey. Movements That Heal: Rhythmic Movement Training and Primitive Reflex Integration. Brisbane, Australia: BookPal, 2011.

Bradshaw, John. Healing the Shame That Binds You. Rev. ed. Deerfield Beach, FL: Health Communications, 2005.

Brown, Brené. Daring Greatly: How the Courage to Be Vulnerable Transforms the Way We Live, Love, Parent, and Lead. New York: Gotham, 2012.

Brown, Brene . The Gifts of Imperfection: Let Go of Who You Think You're Supposed to Be and Embrace Who You Are. Center City, MN: Hazelden, 2010.

DeBenedet, Anthony T. and Lawrence J. Cohen. The Art of Roughhousing: Good Old-Fashioned Horseplay and Why Every Kid Needs It. Philadelphia: Quirk Books, 2011.

Field, Tiffany. Touch. Boston, MA: Bradford Books, 2003.

Field, Tiffany. Touch Therapy. London, UK: Churchill Livingstone, 2000.

Frick, Sheila. M. and Sally R. Young. Listening With the Whole Body: Clinical Concepts and Treatment Guidelines for Therapeutic Listening. Madison, Wisconsin: Vital Links, 2009.

Frick, Sheila M. (1996). Out of the Mouths of Babes: Discovering the Developmental Significance of the Mouth. Stillwater, MN: Pileated Press.

Furth, Hans G. and Harry Wachs. Thinking Goes to School: Piaget's Theory in Practice. New York: Oxford University Press, 1975.

Glasser, Howard and Jennifer Easley. Transforming the Difficult Child: The Nurtured Heart Approach. United Kingdom: Worth, 2007.

Goddard, Sally. Reflexes, Learning and Behavior: A Window into the Child's Mind: A Non-invasive Approach to Solving Learning and Behavior Problems. 2nd ed. Eugene, OR: Fern Ridge, 2005.

Golman, Daniel. Emotional Intelligence: Why It Can Matter More Than IQ. New York, NY: Bantam Books, 2005.

Greene, Ross. Lost at School: Why Our Kids With Behavioral Challenges Are Falling Through the Cracks and How We Can Help Them. New York: Scribner, 2009.

Karp, Harvey. The Happiest Baby on the Block: The New Way to Calm Crying and Help Your Newborn Sleep Longer. New York: Bantam Books, 2003.

Kawar, Mary J. and Sheila M. Frick. Astronaut Training: A Sound Activated Vestibular-Visual Protocol For Moving, Looking, and Listening. Madison, WI: Vital Links, 2005.

Maurice, Catherine. Let Me Hear Your Voice: A Family's Triumph Over Autism. New York: Random House, 1994.

Melillo, Robert. Disconnected Kids: The Groundbreaking Brain Balance Program for Children with Autism, ADHD, Dyslexia, and Other Neurological Disorders. New York: Penguin, 2010.

Oetter, Patricia, Eileen W. Richter, and Sheila M. Frick. M.O.R.E: Integrating the Mouth with Sensory and Postural Functions. San Antonio: Psychological Corp, 1999.

Perry, Bruce., & Maia Szalavitz. The Boy Who Was Raised as a Dog and Other Stories from the Child Psychiatrist's Notebook: What Traumatized Children Can Teach Us About Loss, Love, and Healing. New York: Basic Books, 2007.

Sunbeck, Deborah. Infinity Walk: Preparing Your Mind to Learn. Fawskin, CA: Jalmar Press, 1996.

Suggested Reading

In addition to the wonderful books in the bibliography, I also suggest the following:

Beattie, Melody. Make Miracles in Forty Days: Turning What You Have Into What You Want. New York: Simon & Schuster, 2011.

Covey, Sean. The Seven Habits of Happy Kids. New York: Simon & Schuster, 2008.

DeGangi, Georgia A. and Ann Kendall. Effective Parenting for the Hard-to-Manage Child: A Skills-Based Book. New York: Routledge Press, 2007.

Dorfman, Kelly. Cure Your Child With Food: The Hidden Connection Between Nutrition and Childhood Ailments. New York: Workman, 2013.

Williams, Margery. The Velveteen Rabbit. New York: Random House, 2005. (Original work published 1922).

Products

Tactile Box, Home Depot's painting aisle for brushes, etc. and any drugstore or department store bath or kitchen aisle for sponges, gloves, etc.

Balance cushion by Isokinetics. Available at isokineticsinc.com.
Spritz brand of balloons, available at target.com.

Amscan-brand are high quality party blowers. Available at partycity.com.

Assorted sponge shapes, available at joann.com and other crafts stores.

Mini ice cube makers, available at bedbathandbeyond.com and kitchen supply stores.

Therapeutic Listening at vitallinks.net. Search for a trained practitioner on the site.

Therapeutic Listening CDs can also be purchased at vitalsounds.com (be sure to scroll down).

Sprayza brand blow pens, blow pen kits, available at melissaanddoug.com.

Blow string pipes, available at dysphagiaplus.com.

Citra Citrus Sipper, available at floridabymail.com.

Lemon and/or mint extract, frozen gum, and crunchy or sour foods are easy interventions that help with oral fixation, biting, chewing, and chatter. They are available at grocery or health-food stores.

Lycra swing, available at funandfunction.com.

Lycra or other brands of spandex, large pieces, available at spandexbyyard.com.

Metronome, available at funandfunction.com.

Moods of Indigo, CD of relaxing piano music by Danny Wright, available at dannywright.com and amazon.com.

Spa gloves, available at drugstore.com and other drugstores and beauty supply shops.

Discounted vitamins and natural supplements, available at vitacost.com and other supplement and natural food stores.

Spinning, rocking, and other chairs and seating. Virco, a manufacturer of desks and office seating, produces some great products for children who need movement. See virco.com for more information.

Spinning Board available at therapyshoppe.com.

Hokki and Lupo stools by VS America, great for active kids, available at vs-network.com

Weighted pillows, blankets, and balls, available at funandfunction.com

Soothing music with or without nature sounds available at enhancedhealing.com, by Dr. Harry Henshaw.

Websites

Fun & Function has well-priced therapy items and a large variety of weighted objects for deep pressure. funandfunction.com.

Janet McDonald, M.Ed., LMT, CH, is a therapist and educator with a holistic approach to treating learning differences and developmental challenges. janetowellnessandlearning.com.

Kelly Dorfman at kellydorfman.com provides important information about nutrition for kids and adults.

Mary Massery, DPT, is a physical therapist specializing in posture and breathing. Her site includes breathing exercise videos which can be found at masserypt.com.

MedWise Insurance Advocacy medicalinsuranceadvocacy.com provides help to people in obtaining care they may be eligible to have covered by insurance.

Pileated Press, LLC, publisher of recommended OT books pileatedpress. com.

Rhythmic Entrainment Intervention combines scientific research with traditional therapeutic uses of rhythm. Especially recommended are the CDs Calming Rhythms and Sleep Rhythms, stronginstitute.com.

The Spiral Foundation offers parenting and professional education courses with a focus on the treatment of sensory processing disorders in children, and is a great source of information for parents. http://thespiralfounda-tion.org/

OTThrive.com is home of the Thrive Occupational Therapy practice and author Miriam Manela's weekly blog featuring useful insights, tips, and activities for parents and children.

Acknowledgments

Miriam Manela

My deepest thanks to the following wonderful people:

Kean University Professor Mary Falzarano, PhD, whose detailed clinical suggestions and thoughtful advice enriched the text.

Janet O. McDonald, an encouraging mentor, who contributed important ideas about the Hand Hug and Stretch intervention.

Sara Rothschild, whose vital safety suggestions and insightful comments on the activities made *The Parent-Child Dance* more parent-friendly.

Angela Santiago, dedicated administrator at Thrive OT whose ability to keep everything running on schedule is amazing.

Andre Reichmann, the brilliant, award-winning photographer, for the author's portrait.

Lois Voight, a talented artist with an eye for beauty.

Rachelle Pachtman, who advised on the title, and other aspects of this book.

Moshe (Richard) Zwolinski, author of *Therapy Revolution*, for the calming breath and other suggestions.

Proofreader, Sara Rosenbaum, whose proofreading and advice on style enhanced this book.

Talented illustrator Dena Ackerman, whose sensitive, beautiful drawings bring the activities to life.

Kathryn A. Van Horn whose cover design captures the spirit of this book.

Sara Tennenhaus, Thrive OT's former staff writer.

My co-author, book coach, and editor, C. R. Zwolinski, for her outstanding writing, as well as her guidance and encouragement. She showed me that this book could, indeed, be written and gave me the support I needed to make this dream become a reality.

The wonderful children, teens, moms, dads, teachers, guardians, principals, doctors, and other therapists in a plethora of disciplines, whom I've come to know through my work at Thrive OT, with sincere appreciation for their trust in me and gratitude for what they've taught me.

My former clients, "Arielle" and "Maddy," who so generously allowed their poetry and prose to be included in *The Parent-Child Dance*. I am so proud of you!

My sister Karen Zelinger, who was a source of constant support and also proofread this book and helped with the title.

My dearest grandmother Omi, who always believes in me and is the beloved, dignified matriarch of our extended family.

Most of all, to the great and loving G-d, Who, I am certain, is with me at all times, including during the writing of this book.

-Miriam Manela

•••

C.R. Zwolinski

I'm delighted to have been a part of *The Parent-Child Dance*. Thanks to Miriam Manela, occupational therapist *extraordinaire*, who has so generously shared her experiences and expertise in these pages for the benefit of parents and children; to my flexible clients, who truly understood why this special book was my priority for many months; and especially to my supportive husband whose insights and suggestions were invaluable. Finally, last in deed but first in thought, thanks to G-d, Who has given me such a good life.

C. R. Zwolinski

Index

Behavior categories appear in bold type. Titles of illustrations, activities and interventions appear in italic type. Titles of works appear in quotes.

mindfulness, 81, 82
   and breathing, 16, 82
   defined, 8, 81
Moro reflex
   described, 12, *12*
   integration of, 11–12
   intervention for, 14, *15*
   unintegrated, 11, 13, 40
mouth/oral, 19, 34, 36, 50, 53, 67, 71, 73, 74

N
nail biting, 66, 85
needy, 29
   (*See also* The Princess and the Pea child/ Ch. 3)
nervous, 9, 12
Nervous Tics
   9, 24 (*See also* The Child-on-the-Edge/Ch. 2)
noise, xvii, xix, 2, 3, 5, 6, 19, 30, 31, 40, 51
noisy
   1, 31, 43, 45
   (*See also* Heat-Seeking Missile/ Ch. 4)
novelty-seeker
   45 (*See also* Heat-Seeking Missile/Ch.4)
nutrition, xi-xiii, 3, 8
See also food
nutrition therapy, xi
nutritionist, 3

O
"OT Practice" [journal], 8
"Out of the Mouths of Babes" 69
occupational therapy

Thrive Occupational Therapy, xv, xviii, 7–8, 47, 68

Touch Research Institute, 36

touch, proprioceptive, 4

U

unaffectionate

   29 (*See also* The Princess and the Pea Child/ Ch. 3)

V

validation, 89–90

   affection, 91

   body position and contact, 90–91

   play, 91

   through gesture and expression, 89–92

   verbal expression, 90

W

Wachs, Harry, 71

wild, 9, 45, 49, 52 (*See also* Heat-Seeking Missile/Ch. 4)

withdrawn, x

Wu, Robyn, 8

Y

Yo-Yo Button, 71–72, *72*

Yummies, 69